in the shadow of the cross

Ray Pritchard

in the shadow of the cross

the deeper meaning of calvary

BROADMAN
&HOLMAN
PUBLISHERS

NASHVILLE, TENNESSEE

Published by Broadman & Holman Publishers, Nashville, Tennessee

Dewey Decimal Classification: 232
Subject Heading: SPIRITUALITY

Library of Congress Cataloging-in-Publication Data

Pritchard, Ray, 1952–
    In the shadow of the cross : the deeper meaning of Calvary /
Ray Pritchard.
      p.   cm.
    ISBN 0-8054-2341-9
    1. Jesus Christ—Crucifixion. 2. Holy Cross. I. Title.

    BT453.P75 2001
    232.96—dc21
                                                              00-052889

1 2 3 4 5 6 7 8 9 0 05 04 03 02 01

Dedication to
Greg and Carolyn Kirschner
and to Christine, Katie, Stephanie, and Jonathan,
who have laid down their lives
to take the message of the cross
to the people of Nigeria.

Look, there on the mountains,
the feet of one who brings good news,
who proclaims peace!
NAHUM 1:15

contents

Introduction   1

part 1: the voice from the cross

1. Forgiving the Unforgivable   7
2. Last-Second Salvation   21
3. Final Words of a Family Man   33
4. The Forsaken Christ   47
5. "I Thirst"   63
6. Paid in Full   75
7. A Time to Die   89

part 2: the deeper meaning of the cross

8. Where Grace and Wrath Meet:
   What the Cross Meant to God   107
9. He Became Sin for Us:
   What the Cross Meant to Christ   121
10. One Little Word Shall Fell Him":
    What the Cross Meant to Satan   135
11. The Fool on the Hill:
    What the Cross Means to the World   149

12. Our Crucified God:
    What the Cross Means to the Church   163

13. Free at Last!
    The Cross and Our Sin   177

14. Worthy is the Lamb:
    The Cross in Heaven   197

A Closing Word:
    Lingering at the Foot of the Cross   213

Notes   217

Introduction

A FEW YEARS AGO MY BROTHER Alan purchased an unused church camp not far from the Natchez Trace in northern Mississippi. The site covered 110 acres, including a fourteen-acre lake stocked with hundreds of fish. Because the property had been neglected for about five years, everything had deteriorated. The levee leading to the conference center had washed out, windows were broken, floors had buckled, and the cabins were falling apart. Weeds had taken over a once well-manicured lawn. While on an inspection tour of the property, my brother and I bumped into something lying on the ground. I thought it was a log but it turned out to be a railroad tie. We cleared away the brush and discovered a twelve-foot wooden cross that once stood sentinel by the lake. No one knew or cared that the cross had fallen to the ground.

The fallen cross stands as a symbol for the spiritual condition of the church of Jesus Christ in the early days of the twenty-first century. In many places and, sad to say, in many churches, the cross has fallen to the ground. Instead of boasting in the cross, we have neglected it, substituting in its place religious activity and therapeutic language designed to help us feel better about ourselves. If the cross has fallen from the steeple of too many churches, we have only ourselves to blame. A generation ago there was a movement afoot to remove from our hymnbooks all the songs that spoke about the blood of Christ. Thankfully, that movement has come and gone, but the temptation is always with us to minimize or trivialize what happened when Christ died one Friday afternoon on a hill outside the walls of Jerusalem two thousand years ago. It is precisely because the event seems so remote from our modern world that we are easily tempted to talk of anything else but the cross of Christ.

And yet, when the story is truly told, it must be said that Christianity is supremely the religion of the cross. At the center of our faith a dying man hangs suspended between heaven and earth. Who is he? Why is he there? What are those words he is speaking? What does it all mean? I wrote this book in an attempt to investigate those fundamental questions. Although I had been a Christian for more than thirty years, and a pastor for more than twenty years, and although I knew the details of Good Friday quite well, I had given little thought to the deeper meaning of the cross. That simple desire started me on a personal journey that led to this book.

Someone once complained to famed English preacher Charles Haddon Spurgeon that all his sermons sounded alike. "And well they should," he replied. "First I take a text," he said, "and then I make a beeline for the cross." A quick perusal of his sermons shows how true those words are. In the same way I am trying to make a "beeline" for the cross by looking at it from many perspectives—above, below, from the side, and from the perspective of future generations.

I have written this book in two parts. Part 1, "The Voice from the Cross," deals with the seven sayings of Christ on the cross.

Since Jesus knew he was dying, his last words convey a special meaning to us. They tell us what he was thinking and feeling as his life ebbed away. Part 2, "The Deeper Meaning of the Cross," investigates the cross from various perspectives in order that we might behold, as one might hold a diamond up to the light, the many facets of truth that shine outward from Calvary.

I am keenly aware that the greatest minds in history have pondered the meaning of the cross and have shared their discoveries in a river of books, hymns, paintings, and other magnificent works of art. I possess no special qualification to join the ranks of those who have lingered at the cross except that I too share their faith in the One who died there. In 1825 John Bowring wrote, "In the cross of Christ I glory, towering o'er the wrecks of time." Those words remain true today. The cross of Christ endures while the wrecks of time come and go, vanishing into the mist of history.

I am grateful to Len Goss of Broadman & Holman for his help and encouragement on this project. And special thanks are due to David and ClarLyn Morris, who loaned me the use of their cottage on the Fox River while I was finishing this manuscript.

This is not a book of heavy theology. Its tone is scriptural, and its aim is practical and devotional. Christians of all denominations unite around the cross because, without it, our faith is just another religion. I hope by my writing to "lift him up" so that the reader will love the Lord Jesus and remember with new appreciation that we owe everything to the work he accomplished when he died on the cross so many years ago.

part 1
The voice
from the cross

*So the soldiers took charge of Jesus. Carrying his
own cross, he went out to the place of the Skull
(which in Aramaic is called Golgotha). Here they
crucified him, and with him two others—
one on each side and Jesus in the middle.*
JOHN 19:16b–18

*"Father, forgive them, for they do not know
what they are doing."*
LUKE 23:34

chapter 1
forgiving the unforgivable

T HE MAN CALLED ME ON THE phone and said, "Pastor Ray, could I come see you?" Then he told me his story. "My wife left me for another man and when she got tired of him, she decided to come back to me. Everything seemed fine for a few weeks, then she left me again for the same man and stayed with him for a while. Then she came back a second time and I thought everything was fine. Then she left me again and she's been with him for a while. She just called me up and said, 'I want to come back.' Pastor, I'm not sure I want her back. I can trust somebody once or even twice, but I'm not sure I can trust somebody the third time."

How do you forgive the unforgivable? A woman sat in my office and said, "I think I'm going to kill myself." I asked her why. "I don't have any reason to live any more," she replied. All of her friends had deserted her. She couldn't get a job. She didn't have any money. Everything that she valued in the world was gone. She told me about her children—how they had deserted her, how they couldn't care less what happened to her. "When I told my son that I was thinking about killing myself, he said, 'Mom, why don't you just go ahead and do it and get out of our hair.'"

How do you forgive the unforgivable? The man looked at me and he said, "Pastor, you wouldn't believe what I have been through." Then he told me a story that I found hard to believe. It involved a brutal divorce after many years of marriage, a financial collapse, the loss of his job, the end of his career, and lies told about him behind his back that had ruined his reputation. People he trusted had stabbed him in the back. He looked at me and said, "Pastor, do you want to know the worst of it? The people who have done this to me are Christians."

How do you forgive the unforgivable? Sometimes I wish that I could invite people to come into my office and sit for one week. Just to sit in the corner and listen to the people who come through my office. Listen to all the phone calls. Read the letters I get and the E-mail that arrives day and night. Each week brings an unending series of heartbreaking problems. Divorce. Broken homes. Broken marriages. Broken promises. Children estranged from their parents. Parents estranged from their children. Longtime friends who don't speak to one another anymore. People who've lost their jobs because someone cheated them. People who've lost their fortunes because someone did them wrong. Families that don't even speak at Christmastime because they hate one another so much.

How do you forgive in a situation like that? How do you forgive when by definition what has happened to you is unforgivable?

Killing Time

It's Friday morning at 9 A.M. Killing time. Outside the Damascus Gate is a road, and on the other side of the road is a flat area near the spot where the prophet Jeremiah is buried. Up above is a rocky outcropping that, if studied at a certain angle, looks like a skull. You can see eroded into the limestone two sockets for the eyes, a place for the nose, and maybe a place for the mouth. Skull Hill, they called it. Golgotha. It was the place where the Romans did their killing. Friday was the day and nine o'clock was the time. The soldiers were ready to do their dirty work. They were Roman soldiers. This place called Judea was foreign territory to them. They weren't from Israel. They weren't followers of the Law of Moses. They were simply soldiers who had a job to do. And it happened to be that they were on the death squad. They were in charge of crucifixions.[1]

On this particular Friday morning their workload was a little light. Only three this week. They didn't know the names. They never did, and it didn't matter. They were just the executioners. From their point of view, it didn't pay to stop and think about what they did. That was for someone up the ladder. Guilt or innocence wasn't their business. They'd go crazy if they started worrying about things like that. They just had a job to do. And to do their job, they needed two things. They needed toughness, and they needed good technique. If they did a sloppy job, they were certain to hear about it later.

Mob Psychology

So it's 9 A.M. and up the road comes a group of people. The soldiers know that two of the men being crucified are just average, ordinary criminals—the kind you find in any big city anywhere in the world. That's no big deal.

But the third man, the one from up north, the preacher from Nazareth, his case is different. They don't really know who he is. They know it's important because they sense the buzz in the crowd. There are more people than usual. By the way, that was one of the fringe benefits (if you want to call it that) for being on the crucifixion squad. You never worked alone. There's something morbidly fascinating about watching someone else die. The people of Jerusalem, at least some of them, loved to come out and see the crucifixions. Well, maybe they didn't love it, but they couldn't stay away. Some strange magnetic force drew them back to Skull Hill again and again. But today there were more people than usual, a bigger crowd, noisier, rowdier, milling to and fro, waiting for the action to begin.

Up the road comes a parade of people led by a brawny foreigner carrying a cross. That couldn't be the one they were going to crucify. It turns out he was a man by the name of Simon— Simon of Cyrene. The crowd swirls around him, and behind him is a stooped figure, a man not quite six feet tall. Now walking, now crawling, each step an agony to behold. Half a man, half a creature from the worst nightmare you've ever had. He has been beaten within an inch of his life. His back is in shreds. His front is covered with the markings of the whip. His face is disfigured and swollen where they have ripped out the beard by the roots. And on his head is a crown of thorns six inches long stuck under the skin. A shell of a man. A man already more dead than alive. When the fellows on the crucifixion detail see that, they aren't unhappy, because sometimes people got a little feisty when you tried to nail them to the cross. No, they didn't mind getting a person who was almost dead because it meant that their work would be easier.

They lay the cross out on the ground, and they lay the body of Jesus on the cross. He moves, he moaned, he doesn't do much. One hand over here, one hand over there. Wrapping rope around this arm and around that arm. Rope around the legs, probably bent and partially resting on a small platform. They drive the spike on the forearm side of the wrist so that when the weight of the cross fell, the spike wouldn't rip all the way through the hand. A spike in both wrists and then a spike through the legs. With the ropes in place they begin to pull the cross up. Jesus now spurts blood from the raw wounds. "Steady now, boys, steady. Don't drop it." It was a terrible thing to drop a cross before they got it in the hole. They drop it and it falls with a thud. And there is Jesus, naked and exposed before the world, beaten, bruised, and bloody. The soldiers stand back, satisfied. A job well done.

"Get the dice," someone says. "Let's roll dice for his clothes."

Beyond Forgiveness

What happened that day at Skull Hill was unforgivable. That's the definition of what unforgivable is. When you crucify the Son of God, you have done that which is beyond forgiveness. It is truly unforgivable. And yet Jesus said, in his first words from the cross, *"Father, forgive them, for they know not what they do" (KJV)*. This was the unforgivable sin. Yet Jesus said, "Father, forgive them." That leads me back to the original question, a question that is not just theological or historical, but a question that many of us wrestle with every day: How do you forgive the unforgivable? How do you forgive someone who has done something so terrible that it defies any attempt at human forgiveness?

As I study this story, especially as I study the remarkable words of Jesus, two things come to mind that will help us understand how to forgive the unforgivable.

1. It is possible to forgive the unforgivable by remembering that the people who are hurting you do not really know what they are doing.

If ever a statement seems to be obviously wrong, this is it. An immediate objection comes to mind: "You don't understand. They knew exactly what they were doing. They knew what they were doing before they did it. They knew they were going to hurt me, and they went ahead and did it anyway." When she told that lie she knew what she was doing. When he double-crossed me he knew what he was doing. When he stepped out on me he knew what he was doing. When he broke the marriage vows he knew what he was doing. She knew what she was doing. They knew exactly what they were doing. How can you even bring up that subject? They knew they would hurt me, and they did it on purpose. How can you say they didn't know what they were doing?

Consider Jesus. Who was he talking about when he said, "For they know not what they are doing?" Who is the "they" in that phrase? Perhaps it refers to the Roman soldiers. Did the Roman soldiers know what they were doing or not? Well, yes they knew they were crucifying a man. Did they know who he was? No, they didn't really know who he was. If anybody really didn't know what they were doing, it was the Roman soldiers. It was just a job to them, just the next grisly item on the Friday agenda. To them crucifixion was what their commander ordered them to do. "Hand me the nails. Crucify this guy and get him out of here." That was just a job to them. Surely they didn't really know what they were doing.

Who else is the "they"? What about Pontius Pilate, the Roman governor? Did Pilate know what he was doing? Or to use a modern phrase, What did he know and when did he know it? Pilate knew that Jesus was called the King of the Jews. He knew that Jesus claimed to have authority from heaven. He knew that Jesus was unlike anyone else who had ever come before him. That's what Pilate knew. And what he knew scared him to death, and he tried to wash his hands of it. But he didn't know the whole story.

What about Caiaphas? Caiaphas knew that Jesus was called the Son of God, the Messiah. What did Caiaphas do? He said, "I want nothing to do with this man. Crucify him and get him out of here." Annas? The same way. What about Judas? Didn't Judas know what he was doing? He was with Jesus for three and a half years. But if anything is clear from the New Testament, it is that Judas was totally confused about who Jesus was. He knew that Jesus was supposed to be the Messiah, but it appears that Judas thought Jesus was going to roll into Jerusalem, take over the place, and set himself up as king. Judas was baffled because Jesus didn't fit his preconceptions about what the Messiah was going to do. That's one of the reasons he betrayed him—because he was confused and disillusioned and disappointed at the end. And so it goes with everyone connected with the crucifixion of Jesus. Each person knew a little bit of the story, but none of them really had the big picture. To make it clearer, we can certainly say that the Jewish leaders *thought* they understood Jesus, but they didn't.

Does that mean that these men (and their followers) are not guilty? Not at all. Each person involved in the death of Jesus is morally culpable. There is plenty of guilt to go round. Judas was guilty. Pilate was guilty. Caiaphas was guilty. Annas was guilty.

The Roman soldiers were guilty and so were the Jewish leaders, the Pharisees, and the scribes who conspired to put him to death. And what about the mob? Yes, they were guilty. And what about the spectators who came to cheer and laugh and to mock? Yes, they were guilty, too.

But still we can't escape those haunting words: *"Father, forgive them, for they do not know what they are doing."* Underline the word *what*, because it is the key to the first saying of Christ from the cross. The key is not *the fact* that they do not know. The key is *what*. They do not know *what* they are doing. *They know what they are doing, but they do not know what it really means.* They know what they are doing, but they don't know who the man on the cross really is. They know what they are doing, but they don't grasp the ramifications. That is to say, they are guilty of killing a man, but they are guilty of much worse than they know. *They are guilty of killing the Son of God from heaven.* When Jesus cried out, "Father, forgive them, for they know not what they do," he was really saying, "Father, forgive them because they need forgiveness more than they know." "Father forgive them because they are in desperate need of forgiveness and they don't even know it."

The same is true with the people who hurt you. They need forgiveness more than they know. It's true, they knew what they were doing when they made that telephone call or when they wrote that letter, when they said that thing that tore into your heart, when they left and walked out. They knew exactly what they were doing, but they didn't know the enormity of it. They didn't know how bad and how terrible it was. They only knew on the surface. They didn't know down deep and they can never know down deep, how badly, they hurt you. The people who have hurt you need your forgiveness more than they need anything else in the world. They need it more than they know. And they will probably never change until they get it. And some of them won't change even after they get it. But still you have to forgive them.

That's the deeper meaning of this first word from the cross. *You can forgive the unforgivable if you remember that the people who have hurt you so deeply don't at the deepest level know what they have really done to you.* Forgiveness is what they need, and you are the only one who can give it to them.

If we probe a bit deeper, we discover another truth that flows from these amazing words of Jesus. If the first truth touches how we view others, this one touches how we view ourselves.

2. It is possible to forgive the unforgivable by remembering that Jesus forgave us when we were unforgivable.

This is where the words of Jesus become very personal. *We're included in his prayer.* When he prayed, "Father, forgive them, for they know not what they do," who was included in "them"? The soldiers, the mob, the women, the disciples, Pilate, Caiaphas, Annas, Judas, Peter, and all the Jewish leaders. But that doesn't exhaust this statement. You were included in the "them," and so was I. He was praying for you, and he was praying for me. "No. No. You don't understand. I'm not like those people. I'm different. I'm not that bad. I'm not the kind of person who could crucify anyone. I'd never do anything like that." Oh, yes you are, and yes you would, and yes you have many times, and yes you will again. You're not as good as you look. If you had been there you would have been holding the nails. If you had been there you would have been clapping and cheering. If you had been there you would have been saying, "Crucify him. Crucify him. Stick it to him again. Another nail. Let him have it." We're not that much different. We're not that much better.

At this point we discover a hard reality that keeps us from forgiving the people who hurt us. At the root, it is this: *We think we're better than they are.* We think we would never hurt anybody the way they have hurt us. "I'm just not as bad as that. I'd never treat anybody the way they treated me." We get angry because we think that we would never do to another person what they have done to us. How foolish. How false. How deluded we are when we think that way. It is our false pride that keeps us from the hard step of forgiving the unforgivable.

Not So Good, Not So Nice

It's not as if we are all good and the people who hurt us are all bad. It's not as if we are all pure and they're all evil. It's not as if we've got all of life wired together and they're just a bunch of fools. It's not as if we're totally in the right and they're totally in the wrong. That's not the way the world really works. It's not as if we know all the answers. We're not as good as we think we are and we're not as righteous as we think we are.

Eventually the searing truth hits home even though we would rather avoid it. *We get mad just like they do.* We lose our temper, just like they do. We write stinging letters just like they do. We say stupid things at Christmastime just like they do. We slap our friends just like they do. We hurt our children just like they do. We crucify our enemies just like they do. We break our promises just like they do.

If the truth be told and told fairly, we're just like them. But even that's not quite right. *We are them, and they are us, and if we don't see that, we've missed the real point of Jesus' first cry from the cross.* If we think we're so much better than the people who have hurt us so deeply, we are self-deceived. If only we could see that we're all in the same boat together. We're all truly sinners in one way or another. We all fail in many ways. They fail in one way, and we fail in another.

An Oasis of Forgiveness

It would keep us from being so angry if we could see ourselves the way we really are. If we would admit that we really don't know it all. If we would admit that we really don't have it all together. If we would admit we're not as good as we think we are. We're not as together as we pretend to be. If we'd ever admit the truth, we'd find it easier to forgive the people who have hurt us in an unforgivable way.

The secret of forgiveness is to understand that in the ultimate sense, between you and the person who hurt you, there's really no difference at all. None whatsoever. It is possible to forgive the unforgivable, but you've got to realize before you do it that Jesus forgave you when you were unforgivable. When he prayed that prayer, he wasn't just praying for them back there; he was praying for all of us two thousand years later.

I think it is enormously significant that the first word from the cross is a word of forgiveness. These words teach us that Jesus came to establish a religion of forgiveness. *He is at heart a man of forgiveness.* He came into this world to establish a church that would be an oasis of forgiveness. And to bring to the world a race of forgiving men and women.

Forgiven . . . Forgiven . . . Forgiven

Would you like to become more like Jesus? I suggest you start where Jesus started—by forgiving the people who have hurt you so deeply. I do not for a moment mean to suggest that this is easy. To forgive us cost Jesus his life. To forgive others will cost us something too. We will certainly have to give up our anger, turn away from our bitterness, and decide by a conscious choice that we will forgive those who have sinned against us. And very often we will have to perform that act of forgiveness over and over again until we learn the grace of continual forgiveness.

Every year in January we talk about "turning over a new leaf." For many people that means taking all the leaves from last year and raking them over into a new year. We brought them all with us. We didn't turn anything over; we just carried our burdens and our hurts from one year to the next—haunting memories, injured feelings, and thoughts about the past that we can't get out of our minds. Some people live for years under a terrible burden of remembered pain from the past. At some point we need to let go.

Here's a simple exercise that may help. Take a sheet of paper and write the words of Jesus at the top: "Father, forgive them, for they know not what they do." On the left side of the paper, write down the things and the people and the memories from the past that have hurt you so badly. Make it brief and simple. No one ever needs to see this card. When you are finished, add one word in large letters to the right of each hurt from the past: *Forgiven . . . Forgiven . . . Forgiven.*

And when you're finished, take that paper and rip it up. Don't keep it. Rip it into a dozen pieces and then burn the pieces in the fireplace. *Forgiven . . . Forgiven . . . Forgiven . . . Forgiven . . . Forgiven . . . Forgiven.* Let go of those awful memories once and for all.

This isn't a magical exercise that can suddenly take away your pain, but it is a practical way of coming to grips with the first words from the cross. Do you want to be set free? Would you like to come closer to Jesus Christ than you've ever come before?

Then start where Jesus began on the cross—by becoming a great forgiver.

All of us know that it is easier to talk about forgiveness than it is to do it. And if we are honest, we all know how much we suffer when we forget to do what Jesus did on the cross. We need courage to take the giant step of forgiveness. However painful forgiveness may be, it is infinitely better than refusing to forgive. We will be helped to do it when we remember that Jesus forgave us when we were unforgivable.

Going Deeper

1. According to 1 John 1:7, what does the blood of Jesus Christ do for us?

2. Do you agree that when people hurt us deeply, they don't know what they are doing? Why is that perspective important in the whole issue of forgiveness?

3. How would you answer someone who says, "I won't forgive because I don't want other people to walk all over me"?

4. Which is harder—to forgive or to refuse to forgive? Why?

5. Can you think of anyone whose sin against you seems so great that you regard it as unforgivable? In light of the first saying from the cross, what do you plan to do about that unforgivable sin?

6. Memorize Ephesians 4:32 this week. Ask God to show you any bitterness you are harboring toward others.

A Truth to Remember: *To forgive us cost Jesus his life. To forgive others will cost us something too.*

*"I tell you the truth,
today you will be with me in paradise."*
LUKE 23:43

chapter 2
Last-second salvation

IT IS FRIDAY IN JERUSALEM. THE
smell of death is in the air. Outside the city wall, just north of
the Damascus Gate, in a place long reserved for public execu-
tions, three crosses stand beside a road. A crowd has gathered
this day. Not that crucifixion was unusual. But this day is different. An unusual man is being crucified.

He wasn't an ordinary criminal—not a thief or a murderer or
a pickpocket. In fact, there were those who thought he wasn't
guilty at all. But no matter. There he was on the middle cross. On
either side, two men were crucified with him.

A Portrait of Two Thieves

Who were they? The translators use different words to
describe them . . . *thieves, robbers, malefactors, bandits.* Luke's word

refers to members of the criminal class. It was used for professional criminals and members of the underworld. These men
were hoods, thugs, cutthroat killers, men who killed for fun and
profit—assassins. Tradition suggests that these men were political revolutionaries bent on overthrowing the yoke of Roman
rule. If so, we ought to think of them as ruthless men who
thought nothing of using violence to achieve their political
aims. Beyond that, we know little else about them. We do not
know their names or their hometowns or the specific crime they
committed. We assume that they had been partners in crime, but
that is not certain. Some suggest they were brothers, but there is
no way to be sure. We would not know them at all except for
this: They are supporting players in the greatest drama of all
time, the crucifixion of Jesus Christ.

It may appear that these two men are exactly alike. They were
both criminals who were sentenced to die together at the same
time at the same place on the same day. Both had been severely
beaten before they were crucified, both were stripped naked
before the leering crowd, both were covered with blood and dirt.
Both men were dying and both would soon be dead. No one
could look at them and tell any difference.

But in reality no two men could be more different. These two
men who were crucified on the outer crosses differed on one
main point: how they viewed the man in the middle. They saw
him differently and therefore asked him for different things.

1.   One man wanted escape, not forgiveness.
2.   The other man wanted forgiveness, not escape.

Amazing Faith

Let's take a closer look at the man who wanted forgiveness. Was
any man ever in a more desperate situation? Brutally crucified, he

is dying in agony for sins he had committed, crimes he had done. He is a guilty man justly punished. He deserves to die, and he knows it. By sundown, he will be dead. His case has been tried, the judgment announced, the sentence carried out. All purely legal avenues have been exhausted. This man is as close to death as you can be and still be alive. Now at the last moment he makes one final appeal to the Supreme Court of the Universe: "Jesus, remember me when you come into your kingdom" (Luke 23:42).

I submit to you that here we have the most amazing example of saving faith in all the Bible. Jesus is hanging next to him, a bloody mess, a sight awful to behold. The disciples are long gone, having run for cover when things went bad the night before. The man's feet and arms are nailed to the cross; ropes hold his body upright so it won't fall off. Every movement is agony, every breath torture. Beneath him and behind him the howling mob screams for blood. They jeer, they hiss, they curse, they spit, they roar like wild hyenas. They cheer as he coughs up blood. They roar with approval when someone aims a rock at a piece of tender flesh. It is garish, hellish, brutal, and inhuman. Yet it is here—amid the blood and gore—that this man comes to faith.

Somehow this man saw Jesus bleeding and naked, and yet he believed that he would someday come into his kingdom. No man ever looked less like a king than Jesus did that day, yet this man saw him as he really was. This is made more amazing when you consider that this man had none of the advantages the disciples had. As far as we know, he never heard Jesus teaching by the seashore, he never saw Jesus heal the sick or raise the dead, he knew nothing of Jesus' great parables, and he never saw any of his miracles. This man missed all the outward signs of Jesus' kingship. Yet he believed.

As far as we know, this terrorist knew nothing of the virgin birth, the Old Testament prophecies, the conversation with Nicodemus, or the raising of Lazarus just one week earlier. The coming miracle of the resurrection was unknown to him. All the things we take for granted, he knew nothing about. Yet there on the cross, he came to understand the heart of the gospel. In the crucified Jesus, beaten, mocked, forsaken, his life blood ebbing away, this thief saw a king and another crown than the crown of thorns.

Saved at the Very Last Second

In that light his words seem all the more remarkable. "Jesus, remember me when you come into your kingdom." By saying that, he didn't mean "remember my name" or "erect a monument to me." He simply meant, "At the end of the world, make a place for me in your kingdom." It is the modest prayer of a man who knows he does not deserve what he is asking.

When you put the totality of his words together, you can clearly see how great this man's faith really is:

"This man has done nothing wrong"—Faith in the Person of Christ

"Jesus, *remember* me"—Faith in the Power of Christ

"Jesus, remember *me*"—Faith in the Mercy of Christ

"When you come into your kingdom"—Faith in the Kingdom of Christ

What about this prayer? It is a bit unusual. But it reminds us that God judges the sincerity of our hearts and not the accuracy of our words. When you go to the doctor, you don't usually know exactly what medicine you need. You just need to go to the right doctor. And he'll make sure you get the right medicine. Likewise, this dying thief didn't know all the right words to say, but what he said was good enough because he said it to the right person. When he said, "Jesus, remember me," he didn't know all that he was asking; before sundown he received far more than he expected.

This thief on the cross was dying for his sins—a guilty man justly punished. He cried out to Jesus, and at the very last second he was saved.

A Promise with Three Parts

How do we know this thief was saved? We know he was saved by the answer Jesus gave in verse 43: "I tell you the truth, today you will be with me in paradise." Jesus answered his request by giving him a promise with three parts.

1. Immediate Salvation. In the Greek the word *today* is the first word in the phrase. Jesus put it there for emphasis. Literally, it reads, "*Today* you will be with me in paradise." Meaning, "This very day, the day of your crucifixion." Whatever or wherever "paradise" is, Jesus told this thief that he was going there *that very day.*

2. Personal Salvation. Again the Greek words are very important. The phrase means something like "with me in a very personal way." It is not, "You'll be at the back of the hall and I'll be sitting on the platform," but, "You and me together, side by side." It means to be in the personal presence of another person. Wherever Jesus was going, this thief would be right by his side.

3. Heavenly Salvation. Paradise is the crucial word. The scholars tell us that it originally referred to the walled gardens of the Persian kings. When a king wanted to honor his subjects, he would invite them to walk with him in his garden in the cool of the day. This same word was used in the Greek Old Testament to refer to the Garden of Eden; in Revelation 2:7 it refers to heaven.

It is a place of beauty, openness, and inexpressible blessedness.

Taking these three promises together, we see what a remarkable thing Jesus is saying. He is promising that this thief—who has lived his entire life in crime—will, upon his death, be transferred to heaven, where he will be in the personal presence of Jesus Christ. Truly this thief received much more than he asked.

What a day this was for that misbegotten criminal. In the morning, he's in prison, at noon he's hanging on a cross, by sundown he's in paradise. Out of a life of sin and shame, he passed immediately into eternal blessedness.

Key Questions Answered

These words of Jesus answer several important questions.

1. *Where did the spirit of Jesus go between his death on Friday and his resurrection on Sunday?* Answer: He went to paradise. That is, he (and the repentant thief) went into the presence of God the Father in heaven. He was physically dead and in that sense, he fully entered into the realm of the dead. But his spirit went immediately to paradise, which is the state of eternal blessedness in the presence of God.

2. *What happens to a believer when he dies?* Here the words of Jesus are a great comfort as we bid farewell to our loved ones. Jesus said, "Today you will be *with me* in paradise." At the very moment a believer dies, he passes immediately ("today") into the personal presence of Jesus in heaven. That is what Paul meant when he said that to be absent from the body is to be present with the Lord (2 Cor. 5:8).

This forever puts an end to any notions of "soul-sleep," the false doctrine that suggests that when we die our souls "sleep" in the grave until the moment of the resurrection of the body. Nothing could be farther from the truth. When Christians die, they go directly to heaven. The souls of those who have trusted in the Lord Jesus Christ for salvation at the moment of death immediately pass into his presence and remain there in conscious bliss until the resurrection of the body at his Second Coming.

3. *When does heaven begin for the believer?* The answer is the one Jesus gave to the dying thief—"today." Heaven begins the moment we cross the narrow divide between this life and the next. Not 50 years after we die, or 150 years later, or 1,500 years later, but *today!* We have the word of Jesus on this. This man— this thief, this scoundrel, this wastrel, this professional criminal, this thug—this man who, if he showed up in church today would scare us to death, this man who, if he moved next door, would make us want to move out, this man went directly from the cross to paradise. If the words of Jesus are to be taken literally, this must be true.

Lessons of Hope and Encouragement

As I ponder this story, I take from it three lessons of hope and encouragement.

1. *It is never too late to turn to Christ.* Sometimes people say, "I'm too old for this" or "I'm too old to try that." Sometimes it is true on the physical level. As you get older, there are some things you just can't do anymore. But no one can ever say that about turning to Jesus. It's never too late to turn to him. As long as there is life and breath, as long as the heart still beats, the invitation still stands.

Those of us who are praying for our loved ones should take great hope from this principle. Sometimes we look at people and say, "They are just too far gone. They will never come to Jesus." Then we get discouraged and stop praying for them. But this story teaches us that no one is ever too far gone. It's true that the thief waited until the very last second, but it's also true that in that last second he was saved. Don't ever give up on those you love. They may, like this wretched thief, waste a lifetime and then at the end turn to Jesus Christ.

Don't despair . . . for yourself or for anyone else. It's never too late to turn to Christ.

2. *Even the very worst sinners can be saved at the very last moment.* Sometimes people make fun of "deathbed" conversions, as if such things never happen. I understand their skepticism because most people who come to Christ do so before they are eighteen years old. But it is also true that the door of salvation remains open until the last moments of life. If a man knows that he is dying, is he not likely to be thinking about the hereafter and where he will spend eternity?

I do not mean to suggest that anyone should wait until the last moment to be saved. Far less do I intend to suggest that anyone should live a profligate life with the intention of coming to Christ just before he dies. People who live that way aren't serious about salvation. They are putting off until tomorrow that which they ought to do today. I'm sure if we could speak to this thief who was crucified with Jesus, he would say, "Don't delay. Don't wait. Give your heart to Jesus now."

But the fact remains that this man, who was a very bad man, was indeed saved at the very last moment. Thank God it is so. He had lived an absolutely rotten life, yet he died a Christian death. It happened by the grace of Jesus Christ. I know that some people feel that they are too far gone in sin to ever be forgiven. Some feel so enslaved by their habits that they despair of ever being set free. Many people would do anything to be forgiven, but they think that forgiveness is impossible. Let me put the matter plainly. It doesn't matter where you've been sleeping. It doesn't matter what you've been drinking. It doesn't matter who you've been hanging around with. It doesn't matter what sins you've committed. It doesn't even matter if you've broken the Ten Commandments—all of them, one by one—this week. It just doesn't matter. You can be saved right now.

If this man can be saved, anybody can be saved. If there's hope for him, there's hope for you. If he can make it to heaven, so can you. If Jesus would take him, he'll certainly take you.

3. *God has made salvation simple so every person can be saved.* Consider what we have in this story:

- Salvation independent of the sacraments. This man was never baptized, never took the Lord's Supper, and never went to confession. But he made it to heaven. Therefore, we know you don't have to be baptized or take the Lord's Supper or go to confession in order to be saved.

- Salvation independent of the church. This man never went to church, never walked an aisle during a public invitation, never attended catechism class, and never gave his money to the Lord's work. But he made it to heaven. Therefore, we know that you don't have to go to church, walk an aisle, attend catechism class, or give your money in order to be saved.

- Salvation independent of good works. This man could not lift a hand for the Savior, for his hands were nailed to a cross. He could not run any errands for the Lord, for his feet were nailed to a cross. He could not give his money, for he had not a penny to his name. For this man, there was no way in but the mercy of God.

He was pardoned before he lived a single righteous day. In one transforming moment, a man who was not fit to live on earth was made fit to live in heaven.

"There May I, Though Vile as He"

I take my stand with him. I claim the same mercy. We all get to heaven the same way—by the grace and mercy of God. Over two hundred years ago there was a man in England by the name of William Cowper. He had a nervous disposition and often struggled with bouts of severe depression. At one point he became extremely depressed, fearing that he was under the wrath of God. "I flung myself into a chair by the window and there saw the Bible on the table by the chair. I opened it up and my eyes fell on Romans 3:25, which says of Christ, 'Whom God has made a propitiation through faith in his blood' (paraphrase of KJV). Then and there, I realized what Christ's blood had accomplished and I realized the effects of his atonement for me. I realized God was willing to justify me, and then and there, I trusted Jesus Christ and a great burden was lifted from my soul."

Looking back on that day, William Cowper wrote a hymn that we still sing today. It includes a verse about the dying thief who came to Christ.

> There is a fountain filled with blood,
> Drawn from Immanuel's veins.
> And sinners plunged beneath that flood
> Lose all their guilty stains.
>
> The dying thief rejoiced to see,
> That fountain in his day.
> And there may I, though vile as he,
> Wash all my sins away.

All that God wants from us . . . and all that he will accept . . . is simple faith in his son, Jesus Christ. When we place our faith in Jesus Christ, in that very moment we are saved.

The question is simple. Are you ready to die? You have nothing to fear if you know the Lord. You are not ready to die if you don't. Do you know him? What will you do if you don't know him?

Going Deeper

1. Read 2 Corinthians 5:8 and Philippians 1:21–23. What do these verses teach regarding where Christians go when they die?

2. What do we learn from the fact that one thief was saved and the other was lost?

3. How should this story encourage us as we pray for our lost friends to come to Christ?

4. How would you respond to someone who says, "I want to live it up. I've got plenty of time to be saved"?

5. How much about Christ must a person understand in order to be saved? How much did the dying thief understand?

6. If God has made salvation simple so that everyone can be saved, why aren't all people saved?

A Truth to Remember: *For those who believe in Jesus, heaven begins the moment we cross the narrow divide between this life and the next.*

"When Jesus saw his mother there, and the disciple whom he loved standing nearby, he said to his mother, 'Dear woman, here is your son,' and to the disciple, 'Here is your mother.'"
JOHN 19:26–27

chapter 3
final words of a family man

THIS IS THE THIRD SAYING OF Jesus as he hung on the cross. It is sometime between 9 A.M. and 12 noon on Friday in Jerusalem. A raucous crowd has gathered at Skull Hill to watch the goings-on.

"Near the cross of Jesus stood his mother, his mother's sister, Mary the wife of Clopas, and Mary Magdalene. When Jesus saw his mother there, and the disciple whom he loved standing nearby, he said to his mother, 'Dear woman, here is your son,' and to the disciple, 'Here is your mother.' From that time on, this disciple took her into his home" (John 19:25–27).

I remember the first time I realized my mother was growing old. My family went with me as we traveled to Alabama for my mother's seventieth birthday. We left on Sunday evening and drove through the night, through Indiana, Kentucky, and Tennessee, and got to Alabama early Monday morning not too much the worse for the wear. My wife and I spent Monday resting, but our boys immediately went down to the pier and went fishing. They were not successful for the first several hours until my older brother went down to help them out. He advised them that if you want to catch fish it always helps to put some bait on the hooks. Once they did that, the fish really started biting.

That night we had the big celebration for my mom, including a catered meal and cake baked by her two granddaughters. Concerning their culinary efforts, it could be fairly said that you couldn't find one like it in a bakery anywhere. They baked a yellow cake with chocolate icing and used a candle that kept relighting itself each time you blow it out. After the meal we gave my mother her gifts. She sat at the end of the table with tears in her eyes, smiling about everything. Then we made a few jokes about her age and told some family stories. We had a great time. At the end, my brothers asked me to propose the birthday toast. They chose me because, as someone noted, among all the brothers I'm the one who can talk the longest with the least preparation.

I spent some time the next two days just watching my mother. I hadn't seen her in over a year. That was nearly a decade ago and she had just reached her seventieth birthday. That's the biblical length of life. At that point in life you certainly have to wonder how many years are left. When you're a kid you never think of your parents growing old. You don't know how old they are, but you think whatever age they are, they'll be that age forever. When you're young it's hard to picture your parents getting old. There's nothing wrong with growing old. That's the natural course of life. It's going to happen to all of us if we live long enough. But it's hard to think about your mother or your father growing old. We don't really have a category for that when we're kids.

Silver Threads Among the Gold

I looked at my mother and saw the gray hair around her temples, her face etched with the passing of the years. When she would reach out her hands there was just a little shakiness. I watched as she would walk from room to room. My mother basically was in good health back then, but she was careful when she walked just to make sure she was OK. I hadn't really noticed my mother doing that before. When she took the grandchildren shopping the next day, I went with her. When we got back to the house, the girls went outside to play while the boys went fishing. I noticed my mother resting on the couch because her feet were hurting. I couldn't remember her doing that before, but she hadn't been seventy before, either.

It reminds me of what the Bible says in Ecclesiastes 12:1: "Remember your Creator in the days of your youth, before the days of trouble come and the years approach when you will say, 'I find no pleasure in them.'" As I continued to study my mom I noticed several things about her. The two things she seems to fear the most are losing her health and losing her money. She seems to depend on her children now the way we used to depend on her. When she talks about the future, it's always in terms of the past. It's hard for me to explain unless you already know what I mean. Everything to come is measured in terms of what has already been.

The Keepers of the House

Ecclesiastes 12 speaks of the days of trouble, before the sun and the light and the moon and the stars grow dark and the clouds return after the rain. Solomon goes on to describe the slow deterioration of the body in the declining years of life. The keepers of the house crumble (the arms), the legs grow weary and strong men stoop. The grinders cease because they are few. Those looking through the windows grow dim. The doors to the street are closed and the sound of grinding fades. Men rise up at the sound of birds because they cannot sleep at night. But all their songs grow faint. They can't sing anymore. Men are afraid of heights and dangers in the street. Then man goes to his eternal home and mourners go about the streets.

There's nothing wrong with that. Growing old is part of the normal process of life. It happens to all of us sooner or later, and if it doesn't, that simply means we didn't live long enough to grow old. But it's hard to look at your mother and see her growing old right before your eyes. It seems like just yesterday when it would snow (once every four years or so in Alabama), we'd get the sled out, and Dad would push us down the hill, and Mom would be at the bottom of the hill clapping and cheering for us. The four of us boys were just little kids back then.

As I write these words, my mother is nearly eighty years old. Where have those days gone? Where have all those years gone? It's hard to believe.

Mother Mary

Mary is older now. The years have passed, and Jesus has grown up. Mary has grown older too. She might be in her early fifties. Or she might be fifty now. She could even be sixty or sixty-five. She's not a teenager anymore. She's long past the childbearing years. She's past her twenties, past her thirties, past her forties. From the fact that Joseph isn't mentioned in the crucifixion stories, we can assume that Mary is a widow. Somewhere between the time Jesus was twelve and the time he began his ministry, Joseph seems to have dropped off the scene. Mary's alone now. She's older now. Her shoulders are stooped a little bit. And there are a few silver threads among the gold. The carefree days of youth are gone forever.

She stands at the cross with two other women and John the Apostle. And on the cross, she watches her firstborn son die. She stared in horror as they beat him. She heard the screams, the cries of agony as Jesus was being tortured to death. She couldn't lift a finger to help him. She heard the swear words of the crowd. The blasphemy. She watched as they walked by and laughed at his pain, shouting and cursing and spitting on him. And she could do nothing about it.

Jesus' Last Will and Testament

Only those who have watched a loved one die can understand what it means for Mary to be near the cross on that fateful day. As the hours pass and the agony increases, she looks at her son, just a shell of the man he used to be, beaten almost beyond recognition, writhing in pain. And the crowd loving it. Somewhere during the first three hours comes another cry from the cross. It is totally unexpected. Jesus looking down sees his mother Mary and sees John standing next to her and cries out, "Woman, dear woman, Mother, behold your son" (speaking of John). And to John, "Behold your mother." The Bible says that when Jesus said those words from the cross, immediately, from that very hour, John took Mary into his own home.

We wouldn't understand at first reading the significance of those words. But in Jewish thought the instructions of a dying man were of the same sort as if they were written on a piece of paper. So when Jesus cried out, "Woman, behold your son" and "Son, behold your mother," it is as if Jesus were writing his own last will and testament and executing it right there. Jesus was saying to Mary, "Mother, I'm leaving you now, and I'm not going to be able to take care of you after I'm gone. There's nothing else I can do for you. But do not worry. John will be to you as I was to you. He will be the son you need." "John, do you see my mother? Take care of her after I'm gone. Do for her what I would do if I were still alive."

But why in the midst of all his agony would Jesus say something like this? *It is because even though he is dying in terrible, agonizing torture upon the cross, he is fulfilling the most basic responsibility and the most sacred obligation that any son ever had. He is making sure that someone will care for this matter.*

A Dying Son's Request

What does the Bible say? He was a Jew. He was raised under the law. He knew the fifth commandment, "Honor your father and your mother" (Exod. 20:12). It's not as if Jesus had a lot of options at this point hanging on the cross. He knew that he would be dead within a few hours. He couldn't give his mother any money, for he had no money to give her. He couldn't say, "Mom, when I get off this cross I'll spend some time with you," because he had no time left to spend. He couldn't say, "Mother, in a week or two we'll take a trip together, just the two of us." Death ended any opportunity for more time together. All he could do in his dying moments was to fulfill that final obligation to be sure that his mother was taken care of after he was gone.

Problem Child

I pause here to comment that Jesus had always been something of a "problem child." From the moment of conception, his earthly life had been surrounded by controversy and misunderstanding. The fact that Mary became pregnant during her betrothal to Joseph led to vicious rumors that in one vile form or another have persisted to this very day. Whispers abounded about his paternity. When Jesus was born, Mary got a glimpse of the future when aged Simeon held the child in his arms and said, "A sword will pierce your own soul too" (Luke 2:35). Not long after that came the desperate flight to Egypt to escape the murderous rage of Herod the Great.

Then there was the time when he was twelve years old and stayed behind in the temple to confound the doctors of the law while his parents journeyed back home. He explained himself to his mother with words that must also have perplexed her: "Didn't you know I had to be in my Father's house?" (Luke 2:49). When he grew up, he left his family to begin an itinerant ministry. He was indeed a prophet without honor in his own country. Even his siblings seem not to have clearly understood his true identity. When Mary came to him at the wedding feast at Cana in Galilee, he called her "Dear woman," and not "Mother" (John 2:3). And when someone told him his mother and brothers were waiting to hear him, he replied that all who do the will of God are like a brother or mother or sister to him (Matt. 12:46–50). As he steadfastly marched toward his appointment with death, he redefined his family in spiritual terms.[1]

In calling Jesus a "problem child" I do not mean to imply that he ever disobeyed his parents. He always obeyed them, which in itself is part of the "problem." Jesus was a child like no other child who ever lived. He was truly human and yet truly divine, which is a statement easier to make than it is to explain. Because he was the divine Son of God from heaven incarnate in a human body and taking on truly human nature, he was like other children in some ways and unlike them in others. As he grew up, he began to speak more and more about "his Father's business," the mission of redemption that had sent him from heaven to earth. Bit by bit as he moved closer to his destiny, his true identity became clear to Mary. One wonders what she thought and felt that day at Skull Hill when Simeon's prediction finally came true.

In this saying from the cross, we discover an important and vital truth: *Although Jesus was about the business of saving the world, he was not too busy to care for his parents.*

Application

I draw from this simple story three applications.

1. No one is ever discharged from this sacred obligation.

Our Lord has left the pattern for us to follow. Though you be about the business of saving the world, though you be a Christian committed to spreading the gospel to the ends of this earth, you are not now, nor will you ever be, discharged from the sacred obligation to care for your parents. Not now, not tomorrow, not ever. If our Lord Jesus, hanging in agony, remembered his mother at the very end of his life, then so should we. No one is ever discharged from that sacred and holy obligation.

2. When you can't do anything else for the people you love, you can at least tell them, "I love you."

That's what Jesus was saying on the cross. "Mother, I can't come down. I'll be dead soon, but I want you to be cared for and before I die I want you to know that I love you." Sometimes we use the fact that we can't do all we'd like to do as an excuse for not doing anything at all. In this age of dysfunctional families where marriages are made today and ended tomorrow, where children find themselves spending one week with one parent and one week with another, where the nuclear family has exploded, in a world of broken lives and broken promises, it is all the more important that we do what we can when we can. And that we not delay in hopes of a better day. If we wait to say "I love you" to our parents or our children, we may end up waiting forever. Jesus knew he had only a few hours to live, so he took time in his dying moments to care for his mother. We will rarely have the same foreknowledge of our approaching death. Should we not then be eager to find ways to tell those close to us how much they mean to us?

3. No matter what you do in this life, you can hardly be considered a success if in your rapid climb to the top you neglect to care for your parents.

This may seem to be a controversial statement. Or it may seem like a bit of pious sentimentality. But I assure you it is neither. This is a simple statement of sober reality. It's also hard to explain this to children. While driving home with our two oldest children from a youth outreach event called Sparks-A-Rama, I heard a man on the radio say, "My wife told me that if we wanted our kids to spend time with us later we had to spend time with them now. My wife also told me that if we wanted our kids to talk with us later we had to talk with them now." I thought that sounded good, so I turned off the radio and decided to try a little experiment with my boys to see if they agreed with the basic principle. While we were waiting for the light to change, I turned around to the boys and said, "If we spend time with you now, what will you do for us later?" And from the back came the chorus, "We'll spend time with you later." I thought to myself, "OK, we'll try it again." "If we talk with you now what will you do with us later?" "We'll talk with you later." I thought I'd go for the big one. "If we give you money now . . ." There was a little pause and then Mark, the loyal middle son, said, "We'll give you money, don't worry." Then I said, "OK, if we let you live with us now, when we get older what will you do for us?" And Mark answered, "Oh, you can live with us." At that point Joshua, our oldest son, laughed and said, "Yeah, we'll let you live in a one-room apartment all by yourself." It's a hard principle to get across.

Worse Than an Unbeliever

Here's the principle as I understand it. We all know that the Bible says, "Honor your father and mother." The New Testament says, "Children obey your parents." I think it's true that once you leave your home there will be times you will not be able to obey your parents. But there is never a time when it's OK not to honor your parents. Obey—not always. Honor—always and forever. No one is discharged from that obligation. If you ever use your Christianity as a reason not to take care of your parents, you're worse than an unbeliever. If you are a new Christian and your parents have not followed you in the faith, and if you use that as a reason not to love them and care for them and honor them, you know nothing of what the Christian faith is all about.

We want to save the world, don't we? We can save the world, but while we're saving the world, let's take the time to do what Jesus did. Don't ever use your great calling as an excuse to get out of your basic moral obligations. If the Lord Jesus Christ— beaten, bruised, and bloody—if he had time for his parents while he was on the way to saving the world, then you have time for yours. That's a sacred principle of Scripture.

Three Action Steps

What do you do, and where do you begin? Here are three simple suggestions:

1. If you really want to take this word to heart, go to your parents and tell them you love them.

Make a phone call. Write a note. Or go to them in person and say, "I love you." You really ought to do it. It's been too long since you've done it. *If you're too busy to love your parents, you're too busy.* If you're too busy to honor your parents, you're too busy. If you've filled your life with so many good things that you have no time for the people who brought you into this world, then it's time for a major change. That's number one—go to your parents and tell them you love them. Do it while you have the chance.

2. If you can't honor them while they are alive, you can remember them after they die.

This touches many of us whose parents have already died. What do you do then? The Bible never says, "Honor your parents only as long as they are alive." You are supposed to honor your parents as long as you are alive, whether they are alive or not. How do you do that? Remember them. Remember your mother and your father. Isn't it true that the worst fear we have is that someday we will die and people will forget that we were ever here? One way you honor your parents' memory is simply by remembering what they have done for you. My father died twenty-seven years ago. During my visit to my mother on her seventieth birthday, someone who knew my father said, "You're looking more like your father all the time." I can't imagine a better compliment than that. My father is gone, but I still love him and I honor his memory by remembering who he was and what he did.

3. If you are unable to speak good about your parents, you can honor them by refusing to speak evil of them.

Not all of us had godly parents like Mary and Joseph. Your parents weren't there when you needed them. Perhaps there was a divorce and they left you. Maybe you don't even know where your father and mother are or who they are. Maybe you were abused and hurt by them in the past. And so it doesn't seem possible to honor them outwardly. I understand the truth behind that statement. But even if your parents have hurt you, you are not dismissed from the command to honor them. If you can't do anything else, there's one way you can honor your parents even if they hurt you. You can forgive them and refuse to speak evil against them. Silence can also be a form of honor for those who deserve nothing else.

Dying for Others

It is possible to ponder these words of Jesus and wonder if they truly belong with the other more exalted statements. And yet beneath these final words of a family man we find the very heart of the gospel. When Jesus said, "Woman, behold your son," he was gasping for breath, fighting for life while staring death in the face. Soon the struggle would be over. We may wonder why he called Mary "woman" instead of "mother." No doubt the answer lies in the fact that when he hung on the cross, he was there not simply as her son (though that was true by physical birth) but in a much greater way as the Redeemer of the world. And beyond that, we can add that he was hanging on the cross as Mary's redeemer too. Before Jesus was born, Mary had composed a song (recorded in Luke 1:46–55) called the "Magnificat." In the second line she says, "My spirit rejoices in God my Savior" (Luke 1:47). Mary knew she was a sinner and that she needed a Savior. By calling her "woman," Jesus was signifying that what he would accomplish on the cross would include her too. And by calling her "dear woman," he indicated that though his earthly ties were broken, he still loved her and would make sure she was cared for after he was gone.

In this statement we come to the heart of the good news. Jesus died as he had lived—thinking of others.

His first word: "Father, forgive them"—thinking of his enemies.

His second word: "Today you will be with me in paradise"—thinking of the criminal by his side.

His third word: "Woman, behold your son"—thinking of his mother.

In his final hours Jesus was thinking of others. There is a message here and a call to duty. We must commit ourselves to live the way he lives and to die the way he died. Thinking not of ourselves, but thinking of others. As Jesus hung on the cross, while he was on the way to saving the world, he had enough time to take care of his mother. So must we, in life and in death, take enough time to care for those who have cared for us.

One final word. This story certainly teaches us that the church must indeed be a family. But if we are going to talk about the church as a family, that must be more than a slogan. Why? Because the Christian church was founded by a family man. And in the last hours of his life he was thinking not of himself—he was thinking of his family.

Go and in Jesus' name do likewise.

Going Deeper

A Truth to Remember: *Although Jesus was about the business of saving the world, he was not too busy to care for his parents.*

1. In a practical sense, what does it mean to you to "honor your parents"?

2. Read Ecclesiastes 12. Why is it important to remember God when you are young?

3. Read Psalm 127. In what sense are children a "reward" from the Lord? Why is the man blessed whose "quiver" is full?

4. Do you agree that we are always called to honor our parents, even if we can't always obey them? How can this principle help us win our unbelieving parents who do not understand our faith in Christ?

5. Name three ways we can honor our parents after they have died.

6. If your parents are still living, take a moment and pray for them right now. If you have children, pray for them as well.

"My God, my God, why have you
forsaken me?"
MATTHEW 27:46

chapter 4

The forsaken christ

B ANGLADESH IS NOT A COUNTRY
most of us think about very often. If the truth be told, we barely
think about it at all and would be hard pressed to find it on a
map. It's "over there" on the other side of the world somewhere
near India, but that's about all we know. When a typhoon hit the
Bay of Bengal, suddenly Bangladesh was front-page news. News
reports said that 125,000 people died and millions more were
left homeless. Many people simply vanished beneath the rising
water, their bodies swept out to sea. As the waters receded, res-
cuers found devastation that was almost beyond belief.
Bangladesh was already one of the poorest countries in the world.
Now amid the death, disease, and starvation, the anguished cry
rises from the survivors, "Why has God forsaken us?"

In a hospital room in a major city a little girl lies quietly. She has a strange form of cancer, a strain so virulent that it has her doctors baffled. No one knows how a girl so young could become so sick so quickly. Although they do not say it, the doctors doubt she will ever see her tenth birthday. The little girl's mother tries to be brave, but it isn't easy. In her heart, in words she dares not utter aloud, she wonders, "Why has God forsaken us?"

In the same big city a mother stirs when the alarm clock rings, 5:30 A.M. Another day is beginning. She slips out of the bed and tiptoes to the bathroom. Quickly she showers, dresses, and gets breakfast ready. Meanwhile three children sleep quietly in the next room. Before 7:00 A.M., all four of them will be on their way—the children to a day-care center, the mother to her job. The hours rush by and the sun has almost set when she picks her children up again. Then home, and suppertime, and "read-me-a-story" time, and bath time and finally, bedtime. The children safely asleep, the mother relaxes in front of the TV. After a few minutes, she goes to bed. Five thirty comes all too soon. She sleeps alone. Her husband left her two-and-a-half years ago. Alone with her thoughts she considers her life and asks, "Why has God forsaken me?"

Not many miles away a middle-aged man sits with his head in his hands. Today had started like any other day. Get up, go to work, do your job. Then at 2:45 P.M. his boss called him into his office. "Charlie, I've got bad news." Just like that it was all over. Over after sixteen years, four months, and three days. Over with nothing left to show for it except a pink slip. How will he explain it to his family? What will he say to the guys on his bowling team? Here he is with a family, a big mortgage, two kids who need braces, and no job. In anger—yes in anger!—he cries out to God, "Why have you forsaken me?"

Killing Time

It is Friday afternoon in Jerusalem. Jesus has been hanging on the cross for many hours. On this day more spectators than usual have gathered. Surely many of them have heard about this man Jesus, the rabbi from Nazareth whose fame has swept across the land. His reputation has preceded him. No one is neutral. Some believe, many doubt, a few hate. The onlookers have heard about his miracles, and they wonder if what they have heard could really be true. And they have heard whispers and rumors about amazing claims. Some people even think he is the Messiah. But if that were true, why would he be hanging on a cross? The very thought was incredible and bizarre.

Three Hours of Darkness

The crucifixion had started right on time, at nine o'clock sharp. The Romans were punctual about things like that. At first the crowd was rowdy, loud, raucous, boisterous, as if this were some kind of athletic event. They cheered, they laughed, they shouted, they placed wagers on how long the men being crucified would last. It seemed certain that the man in the middle would not last long. He had already been severely beaten. In fact, it looked like four or five soldiers had taken turns working him over. His skin hung from his back in tatters, his face was bruised and swollen, his eyes nearly shut. Blood trickled from a dozen open wounds. He was an awful sight to behold.

There were voices from all three crosses, a kind of hoarse conversation shouted above the din. Little pieces floated through the air. Something that sounded like "Father, forgive them" something else about "If you are the Son of God," then a promise of paradise. Finally Jesus spotted his mother and spoke to her.

Then it happened. At noon "darkness fell upon all the land." It happened suddenly and without warning. One moment the sun was right overhead; the next moment it had disappeared.

It was not an eclipse, nor was it a dark cloud cover. It was darkness itself, thick, inky-black darkness that fell like a shroud over the land. It was darkness without any hint of light to come. It was chilling blackness that curdled the blood and froze the skin. No one moved. No one spoke. For once even the profane soldiers stopped their swearing. Not a sound broke the dark silence over Skull Hill. Something eerie was going on. It was as if some evil force had taken over the earth and was somehow breathing out the darkness. You could almost reach out and feel the evil all around. From somewhere deep in the earth there was a sound like some dark subterranean chuckle. It was the laughter of hell.

It lasted for three long hours: 12:30—still dark; 1:15—still dark; 2:05—still dark; 2:55—still dark.

3:00 P.M. And just as suddenly as the darkness had descended, it disappeared. Voices now, and shouting. Rubbing the eyes to adjust once again to the bright sunlight. Panic on many faces, confusion on others. A man leans over to his friend and cries out, "What is going on here?"

Mortally Wounded

All eyes focus on the center cross. It is clear the end is near. Jesus is at the point of death. Whatever happened in those three hours of darkness has brought him to death's door. His strength is nearly gone, the struggle almost over. His chest heaves with every breath, his moans now are only whispers. Instinctively the crowd pushes closely to watch his last moments.

Suddenly he screams. Only four words, but they come out in a guttural roar. "Eloi, Eloi, lama sabachthani?" The words (a mixture of Hebrew and Aramaic) form a question that echoes across Skull Hill and drifts across the road. *My God, my God, why have you forsaken me?"*[1]

Take Off Your Shoes

In his book *The Hard Sayings of Jesus*, F. F. Bruce discusses seventy of the hard-to-understand sayings of our Lord. The last one he discusses is this statement. Of these words of Jesus, Bruce comments, "This is the hardest of all the hard statements."

All the commentators agree with him. No statement of Jesus is more mysterious than this one. The problem is not with the words. The words (in Aramaic or Greek or English) are simple. The words we can understand. But what do they mean?[2]

The story is told that the great Martin Luther was studying this text one day. For hours he sat and stared at the text. He said nothing, he wrote nothing, but silently he pondered these words of Jesus. Suddenly he stood up and exclaimed, "God forsaken by God. How can it be?"

Indeed, how can it be? How can God be forsaken by God? How can the Father forsake his own Son?

To read these words is to walk on holy ground. And like Moses before the burning bush, we ought to take off our shoes and tread carefully.

What Do These Words Mean?

Let me say frankly that it is far beyond my meager ability to fully explain this saying of Jesus. My problem is not that I do not have enough space; I have plenty of space. And in the space I have, I will tell you what I know. But what I know is only a fraction of the story. There are mysteries here that no one can explain.

Let us begin by surveying some of the inadequate explanations that have been given to the question, What do these words mean? To say the following ideas are "inadequate" is not to say they are necessarily wrong. It is only to say that they do not tell the whole story.

1. *It has been suggested that this is a cry stemming from Jesus' physical suffering.* Without a doubt, those sufferings were enormous. By the time he uttered these words, he had hung on the cross for six hours—exposed to the hot Palestinian sun and exposed to the taunts of the crowd. He was nearly dead when he cried out, "My God, my God, why have you forsaken me?" Perhaps (it has been suggested) he said that in view of all that had happened to him.

There are two problems with that view. For one thing, the consistent emphasis of the New Testament is that Jesus died *for our sins.* Although the Gospels speak of Jesus' physical suffering, they do not emphasize it. The central issue of the cross was not the physical suffering of our Lord (as terrible as it must have been); the central issue was our Lord bearing the sins of the world. This suggestion tends to weaken the truth that Jesus died *for our sins* and at the same time it tends to overemphasize his physical sufferings.

2. *It has been suggested that this is a cry of faith.* A surprising number of commentators take this view. They note that "My God, my God, why have you forsaken me?" is actually a quotation from Psalm 22:1. In that psalm, David speaks of his own sufferings at the hands of his enemies in a way that ultimately pictures the death of our Lord. Although Psalm 22 begins with a description of intense suffering, it ends on a note of confident

trust in God. For that reason some believe that Christ quoted verse 1 (a cry of desolation) as a way of expressing his trust in God even while he was on the cross.

Unfortunately that view seems to blunt the impact of Jesus' desperate cry. It virtually makes the words mean something like this: "Although it appears that God has forsaken me, in truth he has not, and in the end I will be vindicated." As true as that might be (he *was* ultimately vindicated in the resurrection), that does not seem to be the meaning here. The words of Jesus ought to be taken at their face value—as a cry of utter desolation. And it should be added that these words do not mean that Jesus was renouncing God. Even in the most profound moment of his suffering, he affirms his faith with the words "My God, my God."

3. *It has been suggested that this is a cry of disillusionment.* Skeptics read this as proof that Jesus ultimately failed in his mission. To them these words mean something like "God, you have forsaken me and all is lost. I came to be the Messiah but my mission is a failure." To those who hold such a cynical view, we can only say, read the whole story! Keep reading and you will discover what happens to your "failed" Messiah. Whatever else these words might mean, they are not the words of a defeated man.

The God-Forsaken Man

What, then, do these words mean? I suggest that we will never grasp their full meaning until we see that Jesus was truly forsaken by God. In that black moment on the cross, God the Father turned his back on God the Son. It was, as Martin Luther said, God forsaking God. True, we will never plumb the depths of that statement, but anything less does not do justice to Jesus' words. The word *forsaken* is very strong. It means to abandon, to desert, to disown, to turn away from, to utterly forsake. Please understand. When Jesus said, "Why have you forsaken me?" it was not simply because he *felt* forsaken; he said it because he *was* forsaken. Literally, truly, and actually God the Father abandoned his own Son.

In English the word *godforsaken* usually refers to some deserted, barren locale. We mean that such a place seems unfit for human habitation. But we do not literally mean godforsaken, even though that's what we say. But it was true of Jesus. He was the first and only God-forsaken person in all history.

A Father's Chief Duty

As many people have pointed out, this is the only time Jesus addressed God as "My God." Everywhere else he called him "Father." But here he said, "My God," because the Father-Son relationship was broken at that moment.

Is it not the chief duty of a parent to take care of his children? Is it not our job to ensure that our children do not suffer needlessly? Will we not do anything in our power to spare them pain? And is that not what makes child abuse such a heinous crime? What would cause a father to forsake his own son? Can you explain it? Is that not a breach of a father's chief duty? I ask myself, *What would cause me to abandon my sons?* As I ponder the question, I cannot even imagine the answer.

But that is what God did when Jesus died on the cross. He abandoned his own Son. He turned his back, he disowned him, he rejected the one who was called his "only begotten Son." We may not understand that. Indeed, it is certain that we do not. But that is what these words mean.

In Time and Eternity

That brings us to the great question: *Why would God do such a thing?* One observation will help us find an answer. Something must have happened that day that caused a fundamental change in the Father's relationship with the Son. Something must have happened when Jesus hung on the cross that had never happened before. At that precise moment Jesus was bearing the sin of the world. *During those three hours of blackness, and in the moments immediately afterward, Jesus felt the full weight of sin rolled onto his shoulders.* All of it became his. It happened at that moment of space-time history. Someone may ask, "Does not the Bible teach that Jesus was the 'Lamb that was slain from the creation of the world'?" (Rev. 13:8). The answer is yes. But the slaying itself happened at a particular moment in time—specifically a Friday afternoon in April, A.D. 33. *But since Jesus Christ had a divine nature, what happened to him in history has eternal implications.* I admit that I don't fully understand that last sentence, but I am sure it is true. The death of Christ was a historical event in every sense of the word, but it is historical with eternal implications.

The Trinity Disjointed

Let's go one step further. We know from Habakkuk 1:13 that God cannot look with favor upon wickedness. His eyes are too pure to approve the evil in the world. The key phrase is "with favor." God's holiness demands that he turn away from sin. God will have no part of it. His holiness recoils from the tiniest tinge of wickedness. Therefore (and this is a big "therefore"), when God looked down and saw his Son bearing the sin of the world, he didn't see his Son; he saw instead the sin that he was bearing. And in that awful moment, the Father turned away. Not in anger at his Son. No, he loved his Son as much at that moment as he ever had. He turned away in anger over all the sin of the world that sent his Son to the cross. He turned away in sorrow and deepest pain when he saw what sin had done. He turned away in complete revulsion at the ugliness of sin.

When he did that, Jesus was alone. Completely forsaken. Godforsaken. Abandoned. Deserted. Disowned.

There's an old Southern gospel song called "Ten Thousand Angels." It speaks of the fact that Jesus, by virtue of being the Son of God, could have called ten thousand angels to rescue him from the cross. He didn't do that, and the chorus ends with these words, "But he died alone for you and me." It is true. When Jesus bore the sins of the world, he bore them all alone. Christ was abandoned, the Trinity disjointed, the Godhead broken. The fact that I do not know what those words mean does not stop them from being true. Let it be said over and over again: When Jesus cried out, "My God, my God, why have you forsaken me?" he was really and truly forsaken by God.

He Became Sin for Us

To say that is to say nothing more than the Bible itself says:

1. *Second Corinthians 5:21.* "*God made him (Jesus) who had no sin to be sin for us, so that in him we might become the righteousness of God.*" Think of it. The sinless One was "made sin" for us. When God looked down that day, he saw—not his sinless Son—but sin itself.

2. *Galatians 3:13.* "*Christ redeemed us from the curse of the law by becoming a curse for us, for it is written: 'Cursed is everyone who is hung on a tree.'*" Think of it. When Jesus was baptized, the voice from heaven said, "This is my beloved Son, in whom I am well pleased." No longer would the voice say that. At the cross, the beloved Son became "a curse for us."

3. *Isaiah 53:6. "We all, like sheep, have gone astray, each of us has turned to his own way; and the Lord has laid on him the iniquity of us all."* Think of it. All the iniquity, all the evil, all the crime and hatred of this world—all of it was "laid on him."

Thus did the Son of God make complete identification with sinners. Jesus become a curse for us. He died in our place. And all our sins were laid on him. It was for that reason—and only for that reason—that God the Father forsook his beloved Son.

Emptying the Sewer

Imagine that somewhere in the universe there is a cesspool containing all the sins that have ever been committed. The cesspool is deep, dark, and indescribably foul. All the evil deeds that men and women have ever done are floating there. Imagine that a river of filth constantly flows into that cesspool, replenishing the vile mixture with all the evil done every day. Now imagine that while Jesus is on the cross, that cesspool is emptied onto him. See the flow of filth as it settles upon him. The flow never seems to stop. It is vile, toxic, deadly, filled with disease, pain, and suffering.

When God looked down at his Son, he saw the cesspool of sin emptied on his head. No wonder he turned away from the sight. Who could bear to watch it? All the lust in the world was there. All the broken promises were there. All the murder, all the killing, all the hatred between people. All the theft was there, all the adultery, all the pornography, all the drunkenness, all the bitterness, all the greed, all the gluttony, all the drug abuse, all the crime, all the cursing. Every vile deed, every wicked thought, every vain imagination—all of it was laid upon Jesus when he hung on the cross.

Two Great Implications

I take from this solemn truth two great implications. It reveals to us two things we must never minimize:

1. We must never minimize the horror of human sin. Sometimes we laugh at sin and say, "The devil made me do it," as if sin were something to joke about. But it was our sin that Jesus bore that day. It was our sin that caused the Father to turn away from the Son. It was our sin floating in that cesspool of iniquity. He became a curse, and we were part of the reason. Let us never joke about sin. It is no laughing matter.

2. We must never minimize the awful cost of our salvation. Is it possible that some Christians become tired of hearing about the cross? Is it possible that we would rather hear about happy things? Without the awful pain of the cross, there would be no happy things to talk about. Without the cross there would be no forgiveness. Without the cross there would be no salvation. Without the cross we would be lost forever. Without the cross our sins would still be upon us. It cost Christ everything to redeem us. Let us never make light of what cost him so dearly.

"Where Was God When My Son Died?"

Somewhere I read the story of a father whose son was killed in a tragic accident. In grief and enormous anger, he visited his pastor and poured out his heart. "Where was God when my son died?" he asked. The pastor paused for a moment, and with great wisdom replied, "The same place he was when *his* Son died."

This cry from the cross is for all the lonely people of the world. It is for the abandoned child, the widow, the divorcée struggling to make ends meet, the mother standing over the bed of her suffering daughter, the father out of work, the parents left alone, the prisoner in his cell, the aged who languish in convalescent

homes, wives abandoned by their husbands, singles who celebrate their birthdays alone.

This is the word from the cross for you. No one has ever been
so alone as Jesus was. You will never be forsaken as he was. No
cry of your pain can exceed the cry of his pain when God turned
his back and looked the other way.

- He was forsaken that you might never be forsaken.
- He was abandoned that you might never be abandoned.
- He was deserted that you might never be deserted.
- He was forgotten that you might never be forgotten.

You Don't Have to Go to Hell

If you go to hell, it will be in spite of what Jesus did for you.
He's already paid the penalty for your sins. He took the blow. He
took the pain. He endured the suffering. He took the weight of
all your sins. So if you do go to hell, don't blame Jesus. It's not
his fault.

What is the worst thing about hell? It's not the fire (though
the fire is real). It's not the memory of your past (though the
memory is real). It's not the darkness (though the darkness is
real). The worst thing about hell is that it is the one place in the
universe where people are utterly and forever forsaken by God.
Hell is truly a godforsaken place. That's the hell of hell. To be in
a place where God has abandoned you for all eternity.

That's the bad news. The good news is this: You don't have to
go there. Jesus died a sinner's death and took a sinner's punishment so that guilty sinners like you and me could be eternally
forgiven. If after everything I have said, you still don't understand these words of Jesus, be comforted with this thought: No
one on earth fully understands them. Rest in this simple truth:
He was forsaken that you might never be forsaken. Those who

trust him will never be disappointed, in this life or in the life to come.

A hymn by Ann Ross Cundell Cousin beautifully captures the meaning of this saying from the cross:[3]

O Christ, what burdens bowed Thy Head!
Our load was laid on Thee.
Thou stoodest in the sinner's stead—
Didst bear all ill for me:
A victim led, Thy blood was shed!
Now there's no load for me.

Death and the curse were in our cup—
O Christ, 'twas full for Thee!
But Thou hast drain'd the last dark drop:
'Tis empty now for me.
That bitter cup, love drank it up,
Now blessings flow for me.
Jehovah lifted up His rod:
O Christ, it fell on Thee!
Thou wast sore stricken of Thy God;
There's not one stripe for me.
Thy tears, Thy blood beneath it flowed;
Thy bruising healeth me.

Going Deeper

A Truth to Remember:
When Jesus bore the sins of the world, he bore them all alone.

1. Has there ever been a time when you felt that God had forsaken you? Describe what you learned from that experience.

2. Why was it necessary for the Son to be forsaken by the Father?

3. Sin always separates us from God and from others. How have you seen this principle to be true in your own life?

4. What does it mean to say that the death of Christ was a historical event with eternal implications?

5. Read Psalm 22. Circle or underline every verse that seems to refer to the death of Christ.

6. How would you respond to a person who says he wants a Christianity that emphasizes the ethical teachings of Jesus instead of his death on the cross?

*"Later, knowing that all was now completed, and so that the
Scripture would be fulfilled, Jesus said, 'I am thirsty.'"*
JOHN 19:28

chapter 5

"I Thirst"

J ESUS WAS NEARLY DEAD. THAT
much was clear to everyone. He might live another few minutes,
or possibly another hour—but that was unlikely. Every tortured
breath testified that the Roman soldiers had done their job well.

It had all gone according to plan, more or less. The two criminals and this man Jesus. Nine o'clock came. Crucifixion time.
Hammers and nails. Screams of pain. Gasps. Men stripped
naked. Bugs and flies everywhere. The heat beating down. Sweat
rolling off the bodies. Blood oozing and dripping. The stench
and smell of death. And talking, laughing. "Here he is. King of
the Jews." For three hours it was like any other crucifixion. Then
at high noon came the three hours of total darkness. The sound
of panic. People shouting. Then silence. Thick, oppressive
silence upon the land. Three hours pass, an eternity of darkness.

Suddenly the light shines. There on the center cross was Jesus. He was clearly about to die. Every breath now is a huge effort. Heaving, gasping, fighting for oxygen. Resting upon the nail holes while he inhales. Sweat pouring off of him. Making some strange guttural noises. The experienced soldiers had heard it before—the death rattle. With one last gasp a sound comes out. You can barely hear it more than two or three feet away. More like a moan. It is one word in Greek, two words in English—"*I thirst.*" One of the soldiers motioned for the pail filled with water and sour vinegar. It was the cheapest drink of that day. It was the drink of the common man. It was the drink of the Roman soldier. Whenever the soldiers went out to do their work, they carried it with them in what would be their version of the canteen.

Almost Dead

So the soldiers got the wine, took a sponge, dipped it into the sour vinegar wine, and put it on a stalk of the hyssop. Even the hyssop has meaning. In the Book of Exodus it was the hyssop plant that was dipped in blood, and the blood of the lamb was put on the doorpost. Now the hyssop is used again in a biblical story. The sponge dipped in the sour wine is put on it. The soldier stretches it out. In those days they didn't crucify people very far off the ground. And so with the stalk, which would be about eighteen to twenty-four inches long, a tall soldier could reach Jesus' lips. As Jesus licked the sponge, a few drops of sour vinegar wine would come into his mouth. Taken in quantity, it was an astringent that would constrict the throat. But if you drank just a little it would moisten the lips. Moisten the tongue. Moisten the throat. Just enough so you could say one or two more words.

Now Jesus is almost dead. Moments will pass and he will be gone. Having moistened his lips he cries out, "It is finished." Another second passes and then, "Father, into your hands I commit my spirit." He bowed his head and died. In so doing, he fulfilled two prophecies of the Old Testament: Psalm 22:15: *"My tongue sticks to the roof of my mouth,"* and Psalm 69:21: *"[They] gave me vinegar for my thirst."* As Jesus hung on the cross he made seven different statements. But only one of those statements deals with his personal, physical suffering: *"I thirst."*

Terrible Pain

It is not often appreciated that our Lord Jesus died in terrible pain. If you run the clock back from three o'clock in the afternoon—the moment of his death—back to about three o'clock in the morning and review what had happened to Jesus as he moves through those hours—what you discover is that our Lord Jesus Christ has just been through twelve hours of torture. Arrested in the middle of the night. Slapped around. Pushed around. Mocked. Slapped again. Crowned with thorns that went into his scalp. Scourged with the cat-o'-nine-tails again and again and again with those sharp pieces of leather studded with bits of bone and stone and metal. Hitting him again and again and again until the back was shredded. Until you could see right through to the rib cage. They took his beard and ripped it out. They beat him, and they beat him again. They made him carry the cross. They pounded the nails into his hands and into his feet. Not for one second did he have a moment's rest. Not for one moment had anybody offered him anything.

When Jesus hung on the cross he was not the beautiful, manicured Savior we often see in our stained-glass portraits. It is not too much to say that when Jesus hung on the cross, he was a bloody, maimed, disfigured version of a human being.

No wonder he was thirsty. Loss of blood. Exposure. Heat. Exhaustion. Dehydration. He's been on the cross now for six hours. The sweat rolls off him like buckets. It's hot. And the flies are buzzing around him. The crowds taunting him. The blood mixes with the sweat as it pours off his body. In the end dehydration sets in. First there is a fever. Then a terrible throbbing pain in his head. And then cramps in his abdomen. And then nausea sets in. Then his eyeballs begin to dry up in the sockets. And then his lips begin to go dry. Then his tongue gets swollen and thick. His throat feels like sandpaper. The vocal cords swell up. In the end he can barely whisper. It doesn't sound like human words; it sounds like an animal croaking. No wonder Jesus was thirsty.

The Water of Life Now Dies of Thirst

I suppose it is one of the ultimate ironies of the biblical story that Jesus cried out "I thirst." He who is the water of life now dies of thirst. And I call to your attention this fact: Jesus has not complained at all about his physical condition through all the hours of suffering. When they put the crown on his head he didn't say, "Oh, my head!" When they ripped the beard from his face he didn't say, "Oh, my face!" When they scourged him he didn't say, "Oh, my back!" As the old spiritual has it, through all that they did to him, "He never said a mumblin' word."

Now at last Jesus cries out in the last moments of his life, *"I thirst."* This is the only reference he made to all the sufferings he underwent. Why is that? When Jesus hung on the cross he knew that his work had been completed. He knew that he had borne the sins of the human race. He knew that he had done everything he could for you and for me. And having done what God sent him to do—having cared for the needs of others—only then does he make a comment about his own intense suffering.

Was Jesus a Failure?

At this point a strange question comes to mind. Was Jesus a failure? You could make a good case that the answer is yes. *I think you could make a decent case that Jesus was the greatest failure the world has ever seen.* Just look at his life. He was born into an unimportant family in an unimportant little village. He was ignored, he was taken for granted, he was laughed at. When he spoke, the powers-that-be wanted nothing to do with him. He faced nothing but ridicule and opposition and misunderstanding all his life. And in the end he was crucified like a criminal. His sufferings in those last few hours were unspeakable. When he died he appeared to be yet another forgotten footnote in history. Working with the facts on one level, you could make the case that our Lord was a failure.

But there is another side to the story. Is it not true that you can do everything you know to be right and still end up suffering tremendously? Isn't it true that you can walk the path of righteous integrity and still end up having nothing to show for it? You can pray and pray and pray, and your prayers sometimes will not be answered. You can go to work, and you can live by the rules. You can do a good job, and still the day comes when you are fired without any warning. You may save your money for the dream of a lifetime and suddenly have your money taken away from you. You may work and work and work to make a marriage hold together, and in the end it may fall apart though you have done everything humanly possible to save it. Dear friends may turn against you in the moment of crisis, even though you have walked in integrity and told the truth. There's no guarantee, is there? You could do everything right, and it could turn out all wrong.

No Guarantees

Suffering and hard times do not necessarily mean that you are out of the will of God. While it is true that disobedience generally leads to personal suffering, that's not always the case, at least in this life (see Psalm 73, where this is spelled out in detail). We all suffer for our mistakes sooner or later. But often when we face difficulties, they are not punishment for specific wrongdoing. Sometimes they come because we have done something right and it just has not worked out. Case in point—the Lord Jesus Christ. Look at him on the cross. Behold the Son of God reviled and hated and mocked. Watch him begging for water. What has he done wrong? What sin has he committed? What terrible crime has he done? He has done nothing but obey the Father's will perfectly. And what he got for it was the cross.

Are you so sure that the same thing won't happen to you? Or do you buy into the philosophy that says if you do right, everything is going to come up roses for you? It didn't happen that way for Jesus. Why should it happen that way for you? This has profound implications for the way we look at life, especially those parts that seem to make no sense. Your loneliness does not necessarily mean you are outside the will of God. Your poverty does not necessarily mean you are outside the will of God. Your pain does not necessarily mean you are outside the will of God. The broken relationships you've experienced do not necessarily mean you are outside the will of God. Your sickness does not necessarily mean you are outside the will of God. *Fix your eyes on Jesus, and remember that he did the will of God and ended up on the cross.* For him, doing the will of God meant finishing the work his Father had given him to do. The cross was not an afterthought, some sort of Plan B when the religious leaders turned against him. Jesus came to earth knowing that he would die a cruel death, rejected by the very people he had come to save. He was handed over to die "by God's set purpose and foreknowledge" (Acts 2:23). Truly, he was born to die. That was God's will for his life. And he fulfilled it perfectly.

So I ask the question again: *Was the Lord Jesus Christ a failure?* No, he was not. He was the greatest success this world has ever seen. Nobody ever accomplished more than Jesus Christ did. But for him success came through suffering, hardship, loss, and an agonizing death. Are you so sure the same things won't happen to you?

Lubyanka Prison

But the cross was not the end of the story. On Friday evening Jesus was dead and buried, and he looked like the world's greatest failure. But early on Easter Sunday morning, the stone was rolled away, and Jesus Christ came walking out. Dead on Friday. Raised victorious on Sunday. That's the other side of this great truth. Your sufferings may be used by God in a way greater than anything you ever dreamed. God may redeem the hard times you are going through right now to bring something beautiful into your life far beyond your imagination.

A few years ago I traveled to Russia just as the Communist regime was coming to an end. As we drove to our hotel in Moscow, a Russian friend pointed to a big building about fifteen stories tall. I would suppose it was sixty or seventy years old—gray on the bottom and then brown on the upper floors. "What is that?" "Lubyanka," my friend replied. Lubyanka was the headquarters of the KGB, the secret police of the Soviet Union. Just say the name Lubyanka and it still strikes fear into the hearts of the people. In that building in the heart of Moscow, hundreds and thousands of political prisoners have been imprisoned, often held without bail and without a trial, sometimes for years. Sometimes they were held without any formal charges. Some prisoners were drugged, others were beaten, most were terribly persecuted. Many disappeared never to be heard from again. Some were shipped off to concentration camps in Siberia.

As we drove past that evil fortress, my friend commented, "Many of the brethren have spent time in Lubyanka during the dark days of repression." I thought about what the Russian church has been through. For seventy years they lived under a strict Communist system that tried to stamp out the knowledge of God. Communism was avowedly atheist, built on the teachings of Marx and Lenin. In the early days of the revolution, the communists took over many of the Orthodox churches. Some were turned into factories and schools. Many of the cathedrals were turned into antireligious museums of atheism. The worst of it happened in the 1930s under Stalin.

The Pastor's Story

During my trip I met a man who had been an evangelical pastor for many years in Moscow. Back in the 1930s, his father had also been a pastor. The man said that when he was growing up, the authorities would only permit them to have three religious books—the Bible, *Pilgrim's Progress*, and a children's storybook. "We'd be in terrible trouble if we were caught with anything else," he said. "That was all the Christian literature we could have."

Then he told me this story. "I'll never forget the day when I was ten years old and my father was arrested and taken away. His crime was called Political Activity—that meant preaching the gospel. We watched him go away not knowing if he'd ever return. Four years passed without a word from him. We had no idea where he was. One day as I was standing in the yard with my mother, we saw him coming down the road. The communists had let him go." Then my friend added, "I've never forgotten what that day was like. My father came back, but he didn't stop preaching the gospel. He went right back and kept on doing what he was doing before. And after World War II, he became one of the great evangelical leaders of the last generation."

But that's how it was for many of the Russian Christians. They paid a terrible price for their faith. Fifty years ago it looked like the Communists had won. By closing down the churches, it seemed as if the gospel was almost destroyed in the Soviet Union. The attack against the Christian church continued for decades. Christians were thrown in jail for witnessing in public. In many places the only contact with the outside world came through shortwave radio. Many believers copied the Bible verse by verse as it was read slowly on the radio in the Russian language. Things looked hopeless and Communism appeared to have won the day. The church of Jesus Christ seemed a ragtag band of losers. For a while it appeared that maybe Marx was right—that religion would fade away when Communism came to power.

How different things are today. After seventy years of Communism, the people are awakening as if from a bad dream. In great numbers the Russian people have turned to the gospel of Jesus Christ. Now Christians are free to preach the gospel publicly. Today the Bible is widely available. In

St. Petersburg, Christians banded together to give away one million copies of the story of Jesus—most of them either on the streets of the city or in the public schools. The door that was locked tight has swung wide open. No one could have predicted this fifty years ago or forty years ago or even twenty years ago. But it has happened.

Hungry Hearts

On my last Sunday in Russia, I preached at a small church in Moscow. As we were driving back to the main church, my interpreter pointed to a building. "Do you see that? It's the political headquarters for the Communist Party in Moscow. That's where all the propaganda comes out for the whole country. I preached there not long ago." "You did what?" "I preached there." I thought he meant he preached on the steps of the building—an act in itself inconceivable in earlier times. "When the authorities heard about what we were doing, they invited me to come and present my message. So I met with several hundred of the top Communist officials and preached the gospel to them—at their invitation—in their own headquarters." What was the response? "Oh, I tell you they were so happy to hear me. They listened so well, and when I was through, I gave out several hundred New Testaments and answered many questions."

Now a decade has passed since the fall of Communism, and the gospel continues to make progress, often against continuing opposition and a rising tide of Western-style materialism. Russia still has many problems, but after so much darkness, the light has come flooding in.

Who would have believed it?

From Friday to Sunday

Now we are back in Jerusalem. Moments from now Jesus will be dead. A more hopeless scene you could never imagine. *He died in terrible pain.* But his death is not the end of the story. On Sunday he rose in glorious victory. The same Jesus who cried, "I thirst," rose from the dead, victorious over the grave.

Let us learn the lesson well. Your sufferings do not necessarily mean you are out of the will of God. It is entirely possible that you may do everything God wants you to do and still suffer terribly. Even so, your suffering may yet be redeemed into something much greater than you can imagine! Jesus pointed the way when he cried, "I thirst." That was Friday. On Sunday he rose from the dead to become a gushing spring of Living Water.

Are you suffering right now? Do you live in darkness? Is the way unclear, the light dim? Do you feel the pain of those you love turning against you? Fear not. And do not lose heart.

What is happening to you happened first to Jesus. And what happened to him may yet happen to you. Your suffering has a purpose, your pain has a reason, your darkness leads on to a brighter, better morning.

Run to the cross! Cling to it. Embrace the sufferings of Christ. Though this cannot lessen your pain, it may give you strength to carry on. Jesus suffered *before* you; he also suffered *for* you. Child of God, remember this: As Friday comes before Sunday, so the cross leads on to the empty tomb. And there is no resurrection unless there is first a crucifixion.

Going Deeper

1. Read 1 Peter 2:19–25. How does the example of Christ help us to endure when we suffer for doing right? How did Christ respond when he was insulted?

2. What does this saying of Christ teach us about the nature of his humanity?

3. Why did God the Father allow his Son to suffer such indignities and cruel treatment at the hands of sinful men? What glimpse does this give us of the heart of God?

4. Was Jesus a failure? What facts might lead a person to answer yes to that question?

A Truth to Remember: *Fix your eyes on Jesus and remember that he did the will of God and ended up on the cross.*

5. Do you agree that suffering and loneliness do not necessarily mean you are out of God's will? According to Romans 5:1–3, how can the negative experiences of life produce a positive result in us?

6. Read John 7:37–39. In what ways has Christ the Living Water quenched the thirst of your own soul?

"When he had received the drink, Jesus said, 'It is finished.'"
JOHN 19:30

chapter 6

paid in full

U NFINISHED BUSINESS . . . THE
evidence is all around us.

During a visit to Mt. Rushmore in South Dakota, I learned
that the sculptor, a man named Gutzon Borglum, never finished
his work. If you study the faces carefully, it's clear that he spent
more time on George Washington than he did on the other three
presidents. He originally planned to extend the figures of each
president down into the chest area. But he never lived long
enough to see his dream through to completion. His son continued his work for a few months after his father's death, but he
ran out of money. Millions of tourists have visited since then,
but Mt. Rushmore for all its grandeur remains an unfinished
work of art.

A well-known singer appeared with the Boston Pops
Orchestra at a great Fourth of July celebration. The audience

numbered in the tens of thousands. The closing number—a song I hadn't heard in twenty years—was "Let There Be Peace on Earth." The crowd held hands and swayed back and forth as she sang—"Let there be peace on earth, and let it begin with me." It was a moving sight to see so many earnest voices singing what is essentially a prayer for peace. But just a flick of the channel showed how far we are from "the peace that was meant to be." The screen transported us to some faraway land in the Balkan Peninsula where tanks were blasting away at farmhouses and men were marching off to war. It was a solemn reminder that the quest for peace is just that—a quest and not a finished journey. With so much killing in the world, the singer's voice was like a midsummer night's dream. The search for lasting peace on earth is another bit of unfinished business.

He was only fifty-four and in many ways still rising in his profession. While vacationing in Arizona and Utah, he noticed a nagging pain in his chest. When he returned home, he had the doctors run some tests. The news was bad, as bad as it gets. The beloved actor had pancreatic cancer—inoperable and basically untreatable. His life was measured in days and weeks, not months and years. When he died, he left behind a wife, nine children, and millions of fans. Unfinished business? Plenty. No one plans to die at age fifty-four.

That may be our worst fear . . . that we will die before our time. But it happens all the time.

We die too young . . .

Or we die too soon . . .

Or we die with our work unfinished . . .

Or we die with our dreams unfulfilled.

Living an Unfinished Life

We all know what it's like, don't we? All of us have unfinished things cluttering up the highway of life.

- the half-mowed lawn
- the half-read book
- the letter started but never sent
- the abandoned diet
- the degree we never finished
- the phone calls never returned

But it can be much more serious than that.

- the abandoned child
- the job we quit in a fit of anger
- the wrecked marriage
- the bills never paid
- the promises never kept

All of us go through life leaving behind a trail of unfinished projects and unfulfilled dreams. How few there are who can come to the end of life and say, "I finished exactly what I set out to do."

A Dying Man's Final Words

Only one person in history never left behind any unfinished business. His name is Jesus Christ. *He is the only person who could come to the end of his life and say—with absolute and total truthfulness—"I have finished everything I set out to do."*

It was Friday in Jerusalem, and a huge crowd had gathered at the place called Skull Hill. It was on the north side of the city, just outside the Damascus Gate, and located by the side of a well-traveled road. The Romans liked to hold their crucifixions in public places. Killing people in public had a salutary effect on the masses.

This particular crucifixion started at 9:00 in the morning. For three hours everything proceeded normally. Then at exactly twelve noon, the sky went black. Not overcast, but pitch black, so black that you couldn't see your hand in front of your face. It wasn't anything normal like an eclipse. The darkness seemed to pulse and throb, almost like the darkness was a living thing, an evil, mutant creature escaped from some science-fiction movie.

Only this was no movie. What happened was real. For three hours darkness fell across Jerusalem. There were screams, hideous cries, moans, and other unidentifiable sounds. Then, just as suddenly as it started, the darkness lifted, disappeared, vanished, and sanity returned to the earth. One glance at the middle cross made it clear that this man Jesus would not last much longer. He looked dead already. His body quivered uncontrollably, his chest heaving with every tortured breath. The soldiers knew from long experience that he wouldn't make it to sundown.

Then it happened. He shouted something—"My God, my God, why have you forsaken me?" Someone in the crowd shouted back to him. Moments passed, death drew near, then a hoarse whisper, "I thirst." The soldiers put some sour vinegar on a sponge and lifted it to his lips with a stalk of hyssop. He moistened his lips and took a deep breath. If you listened you could hear the death rattle in his throat. He had less than a minute to live.

Then he spoke again. It was a quick shout. Just one word. If you weren't paying attention, you missed it in all the confusion. Then he breathed out another sentence. Then he was dead.

What was that shout? In Greek it is only one word . . . *Tetelestai* . . . "It is finished."

Was, Is, and Always Will Be

Tetelestai comes from the verb *teleo*, which means "to bring to an end, to complete, to accomplish." It's a crucial word because it signifies the successful end to a particular course of action. It's the word you would use when you finish sailing across the Pacific Ocean; it's the word you would use when you graduate from college; it's the word you would use when you pay off all your credit cards; it's the word you use when you cross the finish line after running your first marathon. The word means more than just "I survived." It means "I did exactly what I set out to do."

But there's more here than the verb itself. *Tetelestai* is in the perfect tense in Greek. That's significant because the perfect tense speaks of an action that has been completed in the past with results continuing into the present. It's different from the past tense, which looks back to an event and says, "This happened." The perfect tense adds the idea that "this happened and it is still in effect today." When Jesus cried out, "It is finished," he meant, "It was finished in the past, and it is still finished in the present, and it will continue to be finished in the future."

Note one other fact. He did not say, "*I* am finished," for that would imply that he died defeated and exhausted. Rather, he cried out, "*It* is finished," meaning "I successfully completed the work I came to do."

Tetelestai, then, is the Savior's final cry of victory. When he died, he left no unfinished business behind. When he said, "It is finished," he was speaking the truth.

What Was Finished?

When you read these words of Jesus, only one question grips the mind—*What* was finished? As you survey the commentators, you find that each writer has his idea of the answer to that question. In fact, the answers are as varied as the writers themselves.

As part of my research for this chapter, I looked at my commentary by Matthew Henry, who lived and wrote over three hundred years ago. Although many have surpassed him in details of exegesis, his work endures as one of the greatest devotional commentaries ever written. In his remarks on this saying of Jesus, he lists eight things that were finished or completed when Jesus cried out, "It is finished."[1]

1. *The malice of his enemies was finished.* By nailing him to the cross, they had done their worst. There was nothing more they could do to the Son of God.

2. *The sufferings ordained by God were finished.* Many times during his ministry, Jesus spoke of "the work" he was sent to do and of the "hour" of trouble that was coming. He once spoke of a "baptism" of suffering he must undergo. All those things were ordained by God. None of them happened by chance. Even the evil plans of the Jews fit somehow into God's greater plan to save the world through the death of his Son (Acts 2:23). But those sufferings were now at an end.

3. *All the Old Testament types and prophecies were fulfilled.* Matthew Henry lists a number of examples—he had been given vinegar to drink (Ps. 69:21), he had been sold for thirty pieces of silver (Zech. 11:12), his hands and feet had been pierced (Ps. 22:16), his garments had been divided (Ps. 22:18), and his side was pierced (Zech. 12:10). There are many other prophesies surrounding his death. All those had been or very soon would be fulfilled.

4. *The ceremonial law was abolished.* As Romans 10:4 puts it, "Christ is the end of the law." It finds its completion and fulfillment in him. Therefore, all the Old Testament rules concerning

animal sacrifices are set aside. And the rules and regulations concerning the priesthood are out of date since the Greater Priest has now laid down his life for his people. Those laws pointed *to* the cross. But once Jesus died, they were no longer needed. "The Mosaic economy is dissolved, to make way for a better hope."

5. *The price of sin was paid in full.* Do you remember the words of John the Baptist when he saw Jesus? He called him "the Lamb of God, who takes away the sin of the world" (John 1:29). That "taking away" of sin was accomplished by the death of our Lord.

6. *His physical sufferings were at an end.* "The storm is over, the worst is past; all his pains and agonies are at an end, and he is just going to paradise, entering upon the joy set before him."

7. *His life was now finished.* When Jesus cried out, "It is finished," he had only a few seconds to live. All that he had come to do had been fully accomplished. His life and his mission came to an end at exactly the same moment.

8. *The work of redemption was now complete.* This is undoubtedly the major meaning. Matthew Henry expands on what Christ's death accomplished in four statements. The death of Christ provided a . . .

full satisfaction for sin,

fatal blow to Satan,

fountain of grace opened that will flow forever,

foundation of peace laid that will last forever.

Paid in Full

But there is more to the meaning of *tetelestai*. It means all of the above, but it especially applies to the price paid for the sins of the world. Merrill Tenney notes that the verb "was used in the first and second centuries in the sense of 'fulfilling' or 'paying' a debt and often appeared in receipts. 'It is finished' . . . could be interpreted as 'Paid in full.'"2 "Paid in full" means that once a thing is paid for, you never have to pay for it again. In fact, "paid in full" means that once a thing is paid for, it is foolish to try to pay for it again.

That point came home to me when we visited some friends who lived in Norwood, Colorado. Whenever this family comes through Chicago, they stay with us. And several years earlier we had stayed with them in Colorado. They were delighted when they heard we were coming through their area again on our way back home from a trip to Arizona. The husband told us not to worry; they would be glad for us to stay with them. I assumed that we would be sleeping on sofas for the night—which was fine with us. But when I called him from southern Utah to let him know we would arrive in three or four hours, he said that he had a room for us at the local hotel—the Back Narrows Inn. I thought he was kidding. I didn't think Norwood was big enough to have a hotel. But he was serious. "Our house isn't big enough (they had moved since our last visit a few years earlier), so we'll put you up in the hotel." When I protested, he said, "Don't worry about it. I've worked it out with the owner, and I've already taken care of the bill." That was that. We were staying at the hotel, and he was paying. And nothing I could say would make the slightest difference.

We got to the Back Narrows Inn about 10:00 P.M. and found it to be a small, turn-of-the-century building that had been converted into a fifteen- or twenty-room hotel. When we arrived, the owner greeted us, handed us our keys, and said, "Your friend has taken care of everything." Indeed he had. We didn't even have to formally check in. No credit cards, no filling out forms, no "How will you be paying for this, sir?" It wasn't necessary because my friend had personally paid the price in full. All that was left to us was to enjoy our rooms, provided free of charge to us by virtue of a friend's hospitality.

Now suppose that I had tried to pay the bill anyway. In the first place, I couldn't do it because my friend had already paid it. In the second place, if I kept on trying it would be an insult to my friend, meaning that either I didn't take him at his word or I wouldn't accept his hospitality. If I insisted on paying for the rooms, I wouldn't have stayed in the hotel at all. Either I stayed there courtesy of his kindness to me, or I didn't stay at all.

The same is true in the realm of personal salvation. Either you accept the fact that Jesus paid it all or you try to pay yourself. But who could ever pay for even one sin? How much does a sin cost? How could you ever pay the infinite cost? In the end your only choice is to trust that Jesus has indeed paid in full for your salvation or you reject what Christ did when he died on the cross. There is no third option.

Name Your Sin

So let me ask you a personal question. What sin is keeping you from God? Is it anger? Is it lust? Is it a hard heart of unbelief? Is it alcohol abuse? Is it an uncontrollable temper? Is it cheating? Is it stealing? Is it adultery? Is it abortion? Is it pride? Is it greed? Is it homosexuality? Is it racial prejudice? Is it a bitter spirit?

Let me tell you the best news you've ever heard. It doesn't matter what "your" sin is. It doesn't matter how many sins you've piled up in your life. It doesn't matter how guilty you think you are. It doesn't matter what you've been doing this week. It doesn't matter how bad you've been. It doesn't matter how many skeletons rattle around in your closet.

All of your sins have been stamped by God with one word—
Tetelestai—paid in full.

Anger . . . *Tetelestai* . . . Paid in Full

Uncontrolled ambition . . . *Tetelestai* . . . Paid in Full

Gossip . . . *Tetelestai* . . . Paid in Full

Drunkenness . . . *Tetelestai* . . . Paid in Full

Fornication . . . *Tetelestai* . . . Paid in Full

Embezzlement . . . *Tetelestai* . . . Paid in Full

Lying . . . *Tetelestai* . . . Paid in Full

Disobedience . . . *Tetelestai* . . . Paid in Full

Slothfulness . . . *Tetelestai* . . . Paid in Full

Pride . . . *Tetelestai* . . . Paid in Full

Murder . . . *Tetelestai* . . . Paid in Full

Bribery . . . *Tetelestai* . . . Paid in Full

Those are just examples. Just fill in the blank with whatever
sins plague your life. Then write over those sins the word *tetelestai* because through the blood of Jesus Christ the price for your
sins has been paid in full.

Three Abiding Principles

*1. Since Jesus Christ paid in full, the work of salvation is now com-
plete.* That is what "it is finished" means. The debt was paid, the
work was accomplished, the sacrifice was completed. And since
the verb is in the perfect tense, it means that when Jesus died, he
died once for all time. The sacrifice was sufficient to pay for the
sins of every person who has ever lived—past, present, or future.

And that explains what theologians mean when they talk
about the "finished work" of Jesus Christ. That's not just a slogan;
it's a profound spiritual truth. What Jesus accomplished in his
death was so awesome, so total, so complete that it could never
be repeated. Not even by Jesus himself. His work is "finished."

There is nothing more God could do to save the human race. There is no Plan B. Plan A (the death of Christ) was good enough.

2. Since Jesus Christ paid in full, all efforts to add anything to what Christ did on the cross are doomed to failure. This is a crucial point because sinners often think there is something they can do (or must do) in order to be forgiven by God. But the death of Christ proves the opposite. No degree of personal reformation (no matter how much you clean up your life), no baptism of any kind, no acts of bravery (not even on the battlefield), no deeds of kindness (no matter what the motivation), no religious activity of any kind can help the sinner take even the tiniest step toward heaven. Sin is forgiven by the blood of Jesus Christ on the basis of his death on the cross. Since Christ has died for us, nothing we do (or have done or will do) makes the slightest difference in terms of our salvation, forgiveness, justification, and full acceptance by God. These are shocking words to some people because almost everyone secretly believes there is something we must "do" in order to be saved. But we can go so far as to say that nothing can be added to the value of the blood of Christ. Good resolve and sincere effort are noble things, but they cannot forgive or help forgive our sin. That's what "paid in full" really means.

Let me put it very simply. If Jesus paid it all, you don't have to. If you try to pay for your salvation, it means you don't think he paid it all. There is no middle ground between those two propositions. God is not trying to sell you salvation. He doesn't offer salvation at half-price. And you can't split the cost with him or pay for your sins on the installment plan. God is offering you salvation free of charge. That's what *tetelestai* means. Jesus paid in full so you wouldn't have to pay anything.

3. *Since Jesus Christ paid in full, the only thing you can do is accept it or reject it.* A few years ago a Nigerian pastor gave me a hymnbook entitled *Sacred Songs and Solos.* When you open to the title page, you find that it was compiled by Ira Sankey (D. L. Moody's song leader) in the late 1800s. This hymnbook—though very old—is still used by the churches of Nigeria and contains many unfamiliar hymns. But some of them are gems. These are the words to number 142:

> Nothing either great or small—
>   Nothing, sinner no.
> Jesus did it, did it all,
>   Long, long ago.
>
> "It is finished!" yes, indeed.
>   Finished every jot:
> Sinner, this is all you need—
>   Tell me, is it not?
>
> When He, from His lofty throne,
>   Stooped to do and die,
> Everything was fully done:
>   Hearken to His cry.
>
> Weary, working, burdened one,
>   Wherefore toil you so?
> Cease your doing; all was done
>   Long, long ago.
>
> Till to Jesus' work you cling
>   By a simple faith,
> "Doing" is a deadly thing—
>   "Doing" leads to death.

> Cast your deadly "doing" down—
> Down at Jesus' feet;
> Stand in Him, in Him alone,
> Gloriously complete.

They don't write hymns like that nowadays. There's enough good theology in those six stanzas to save the entire world. Just consider these two lines—"Cease your doing; all was done long, long ago." It's true. "All was done" when Jesus cried, "It is finished." It was finished then, it is finished now, and to the glory of God—after a million times a million years have passed—it will still be finished.

Thanks be to God that Jesus left no unfinished business behind. He finished what he came to do, and in finishing his work he paid in full the price for your sins. As the hymn says, "Sinner, this is all you need. Tell me, is it not?"

Going Deeper

1. Consider your own dreams and goals. How much "unfinished business" is left in your life at this point? How confident are you that you will be able to finish everything by the time you die?

2. When Jesus cried out, "It is finished," was that wishful thinking or a statement of fact? If the latter, how could he be so sure that his work was indeed finished and that he had completed all that he came to do?

3. Name some of the "Plan B" methods of salvation that people use to add to Christ's work on the cross. What happens when we add anything to the value of Christ's death as a means of salvation?

4. Make a list of "your" sins on a sheet of paper. When you are finished, in big letters write over the list the words "Paid in Full."

5. Take a few minutes to read and meditate on Isaiah 53. What do you learn from this chapter about the meaning and purpose of Christ's death?

6. How would you answer someone who says, "I don't see how the death of one man two thousand years ago can pay for my sins, much less the sins of the whole world"?

*"Jesus called out with a loud voice, 'Father, into your hands
I commit my spirit.' When he had said this,
he breathed his last."*
LUKE 23:46

chapter 7

A Time to Die

D EATH STANDS WATCH OVER THE center cross. It is the middle of Friday afternoon on a spring day in Jerusalem. The earthly life of Jesus Christ will soon come to an end. Things are worse now. More blood. More screams. More gore. The insects swarm around the three naked bodies. There are shouts, restless words from the crowd. Several hundred people have gathered at Skull Hill to watch him die.

It hasn't been an ordinary day. Not that you could ever call crucifixion ordinary. But the Romans did it all the time. It was their favored method for dealing with criminals and trouble-makers. There were plenty of easier ways to kill people—and the Romans knew all about those ways, too—but crucifixion had its advantages, the primary one being that crucifixion was such a gruesome spectacle that it caught the public attention in a way that something mundane like poisoning could never do.

But this time the Romans were crucifying three men on the eve of the Jewish Passover. That meant the city would be clogged with religious pilgrims. The message would come through loud and clear: Don't mess with us.

Things had started well enough. The three men were crucified at 9:00 A.M.—the normal starting time. The crowd was larger than usual, mostly because of the man in the middle, one Jesus of Nazareth. The hard part was nailing the men to the cross. At best it was a bloody ordeal. If the victims struggled (and most of them did), the thing could turn into a gory mess. But the man in the middle had not struggled at all. He looked half-dead before they laid him on the cross. The scourging must have taken a lot out of him.

The first three hours were no problem. The three men spoke to one another briefly, and people in the crowd shouted various things—mostly jeers and taunts. Jesus seemed to have a following of people—friends and family—who came to watch the proceedings. They didn't say much.

Three Hours of Darkness

Everything changed at 12:00 noon. Suddenly everything went dark. The sun disappeared—just like that—and thick darkness settled over the land. It was the darkness of a cave in the middle of the night, thick, ugly darkness that made the hair stand up on the back of your neck. It lasted for three hours. At 3:00 P.M., the sun came out just as suddenly as it had disappeared. All eyes were drawn to the center cross. Something had happened to Jesus during those three hours, but exactly what was hard to say. The other two looked awful, the way men always do when they are crucified, but Jesus was different. Something terrible had happened to him during that three hours of darkness, some awful burden that had descended on him and sucked out what little life was left in him. You didn't have to be a doctor to know that he was about to die.

His chest heaved mightily with each breath, his eyes looked faraway, his voice was little more than a guttural groan, the death rattle was in his throat. Suddenly he shouted something, and somebody shouted back to him. Then the soldiers moistened his lips with a sponge stuck on the end of a hyssop stalk. His head dropped, he took another breath, he shouted one word, *"Tetelestai!"* and it seemed as if he had died. A moment passed, then he took one final breath and cried out with a loud voice, "Father, into your hands I commit my spirit." Then he bowed his head and his whole body seemed to slump forward.

Stunned silence. Followed by, "Surely, this was the Son of God." Shock. "Who was that man?" Anger now, and fear on the faces of the crowd. Here and there, soft sobs and quiet tears. Much later came the spear in the side, but Jesus was long dead at that point.

Last Words

This is how Luke the physician tells the story of the last moments of Jesus' life:

> It was now about the sixth hour, and darkness
> came over the whole land until the ninth hour, for
> the sun stopped shining. And the curtain of the
> temple was torn in two. Jesus called out with a
> loud voice, "Father, into your hands I commit my
> spirit." When he had said this, he breathed his last
> (Luke 23:44–46).

Luke is the only writer to record the last words of the Son of God: "Father, into your hands I commit my spirit." Every word tells us something important:

Father—This was Jesus' favorite title for God. It spoke of the intimate family relationship that had existed from all eternity. His first word from the cross had been, "Father, forgive them." His last word was, "Father, into your hands I commit my spirit." But in between he had cried out, "My God, my God, why have you forsaken me?" He called him "My God" and not "Father," because in that agonizing moment the Father turned his back on the Son as Jesus bore the sin of the world. God forsaken by God! But no longer. *Jesus dies with the knowledge that the price has been fully paid, the cup emptied, the burden borne, estrangement ended, the battle won, the struggle over.* Whatever happened in those three mysterious hours of darkness is now in the past. Jesus yields his life to the one he called "Father."

Into your hands—O the touch of a father's hands! What son does not long for his father to reach out and embrace him? There is something wonderful about this expression. It speaks of safety—"I am safe in my father's hands"—and of greeting—"Welcome home, Son"—and of love—"Dad, it's so good to see you again"—and of approval—"I'm so proud of you, Son."

For fifteen hours Jesus has been in the hands of wicked men. With their hands, they beat him. With their hands, they slapped him. With their hands, they abused him. With their hands, they crowned him with thorns. With their hands, they ripped out his beard. With their hands, they smashed him black and blue. With their hands, they whipped his back until it was torn to bits. All that is behind him now. Wicked hands have done all they can do. Jesus now returns to his Father's hands.

I commit—The word *commit* means to deposit something valuable in a safe place. It's what you do when you take your will and your most valuable possessions and put them in a safe-deposit box at the bank.

My spirit—By this phrase, Jesus meant his very life, his personal existence. Now that his physical life was over, Jesus commits himself into his Father's hands for safekeeping. "Father, I can no longer care for myself. I place myself in your good hands for safekeeping."

"Now I Lay Me Down to Sleep"

These words are a quotation from Scripture. With his final breath, Jesus recited Psalm 31:5 and simply added the word *Father* to the front of the quotation. Jewish mothers would teach their children to recite that verse every night before they went to bed. For many children, it would be the first verse of Scripture they ever learned.

On the cross, as his life is ebbing away, Jesus reverts to the prayer of his childhood, the prayer his mother taught him in Nazareth, the prayer with which he ended each day. *In the end, his strength gone, his body tortured almost beyond recognition, his mind recalls the words he learned as a little boy—"Father, into your hands I commit my spirit."* The prayer has the same meaning and effect as the prayer many of our children pray each night:

> Now I lay me down to sleep.
>
> I pray thee, Lord, my soul to keep.
>
> If I should die before I wake,
>
> I pray thee, Lord, my soul to take.
>
> —Isaac Watts

Sometimes we wonder if our children pay any attention when we recite Scripture and sing to them at bedtime. Often it seems as if our words go in one ear and out the other. But those little ears hear more than we know, and the heart remembers far more than we realize. No one can overestimate the value of patiently teaching the truth of God to our children day in and day out. What seems to be wasted time may some day be the only thing they can remember.

The End of the Story

The moment has come. Jesus has only seconds to live. All that he came to do has been accomplished. It is time to die. Two things happened at the very end of his life that merit our attention.

1. His physical sufferings reached their climax. The pain now is unbearable. Breathing is almost impossible. The crowd gathers around, like vultures circling their prey. The friends of Jesus watch in horror as his life ebbs away. Death rattles in his throat. From somewhere down below, a fiendish, evil howling. The angels look away. The Son of God is about to die.

What was it like to die by crucifixion? It involved a variety of tortures that led to enormous blood loss, intense pain, exposure to the elements, an array of bodily wounds, extreme difficulty in breathing, tearing of muscles and joints, loss of vital bodily fluids, the onset of shock, cramping, extreme dehydration, blurred vision, swelling of the vocal cords, inability to control bodily functions, failure of various internal organs, all leading to eventual death.[1] The final event could come in a few hours or it might take several days, which is why the Romans routinely broke the legs of their victims. They wanted them to die faster. They didn't do that to Jesus because he was already dead. Death on a cross was excruciating in every sense. That's a good word to use because it comes from a Latin word meaning "out of the cross."

Over the centuries skeptics have occasionally argued that Jesus didn't really die on the cross. Some skeptics have proposed that Jesus survived the crucifixion, swooned on the cross, revived in the tomb, came forth on Easter Sunday, and fooled everyone into thinking he had risen from the dead. Just to state the theory is to refute it. The whole purpose of crucifixion was brutal, agonizing death. No one could possibly survive beating, scourging, the torture of crucifixion, and being pierced by a spear. The Romans specialized in killing people. They knew the difference between a dead man and an unconscious man. Besides, if Jesus did somehow revive after so much physical torture, how did he roll the stone away and then give the appearance of perfect physical health on Sunday morning? The theory makes no sense whatsoever.

The point not to be missed is that when the Bible says that Jesus breathed his last, it means that Jesus was literally, actually, and physically dead. The Romans had done their work well.

2. *He voluntarily gave up his life.* This may seem at odds with the gruesome account given above. Christ was arrested and tried like a common criminal. He was beaten within an inch of his life. He suffered the terrible ordeal of crucifixion and died an agonizing death. Surely his life was forcibly taken from him.

Not so. Jesus himself addressed this question in John 10:17–18.

> "The reason my Father loves me is that I lay
> down my life—only to take it up again. No one
> takes it from me, but I lay it down of my own
> accord. I have authority to lay it down and author-
> ity to take it up again."

This perfectly harmonizes the Gospel accounts of the death of Christ. Matthew 27:50 tells us that at the moment of his death, Jesus "gave up his spirit." That is, he voluntarily yielded it up to the Father. His life was *not* taken from him against his will; when the time came, he gave up his life voluntarily. To the very end, the Son of God remained sovereign over life and death. He died in accordance with God's plan, at precisely the right moment, in exactly the right way, accomplishing all that the Father intended from before the foundation of the world. Nothing happened by chance, including the betrayal by Judas, the denials by Peter, his arrest, his trials, his physical sufferings, and the ordeal on the cross. All of it happened as God had ordained.

Was Peter a free man? Yes. Was Judas free? Yes. Was Pilate free? Yes. Was Herod free? Yes. And the Roman soldiers were acting under orders from their superiors. No one did what they did in the last twenty-four hours under a sense of divine compulsion. And yet, everything happened in precisely the way God intended. There is a mystery here that no one can fathom. Those who mistreated Christ are morally culpable for their actions, yet their free choices fulfilled God's predetermined plan. The fact that we do not understand this simply means that God is God and we are not. *Seen from this vantage point, the death of Christ is not the final act of a tragedy but the victorious ending of a mighty battle.*

From all of this we may draw several lessons and applications:
1. He knew it was time to die.
2. He wasn't afraid to die.
3. He died with his life complete.
4. He died without anger or bitterness.
5. He died in complete control of his senses and his circumstances.

6. He died at precisely the right moment and in precisely the right way.

7. He died knowing where he was going—back into the Father's hands.

The death of Jesus is a model of how the faithful face death. They are not afraid. They are not filled with remorse over wasted opportunities. *They endure their portion with grace, knowing that a better day awaits on the other side of the great divide.* If they suffer, they hold fast to the promises of God as their only hope. They do nothing to hasten the moment, but when it finally comes, they have courage to face it for they have committed themselves completely into their Father's hands.

And so Jesus died like a child asleep in his father's arms. Exhausted, weary, having suffered the worst that man could do, he finally yielded up his life and breathed his last. It was a quiet ending, a graceful exit, a peaceful passing from the brutality of this world.

Freed from the Fear of Death

All of us must die sooner or later. Of all the fears that trouble the heart of man, perhaps none is greater than the fear of death. All of our fears can be rolled up into this greatest fear—we are afraid to die. We fear death because it is so final. We fear death because we are not sure what happens when we die. We fear death because it means leaving the world we know for another world we know nothing about.

Men will do anything to keep from thinking about death. They will drink themselves into a stupor rather than face the reality of their own mortality. They race through life going a thousand miles an hour, rushing from one thing to another in a desperate attempt to keep their mind off the inevitable. We fear so many things—nuclear war, financial collapse, international intrigue, cancer, AIDS, the onset of old age—but behind them all lurks the great unspoken fear of death. It is unspoken because you cannot speak of the things you truly fear. They are too frightening for words.

Death is the final enemy. It is the end of one thing and the beginning of . . . what? Modern men and women do not know how to finish that sentence. Therefore we are afraid. Into the breach steps Jesus Christ and says, "Fear not, for I have conquered death." He was there. He died just like all men die. And he came back to tell the story. No one else has ever done that.

These are the words of Hebrews 2:14–15.

> Since the children have flesh and blood, he too
> shared in their humanity so that by his death he
> might destroy him who holds the power of
> death—that is, the devil—and free those who all
> their lives were held in slavery by their fear of
> death.

Who holds the power of death? Satan does. Death belongs to him. Death is his. He owns it. Before Satan was, death was not. When Satan is no more, death will be no more. Between now and then, Satan still rules the realm of death. Men fear death because they are entering a realm Satan controls. But the death of Jesus Christ has spoiled Satan's power. As long as men stayed dead, death was Satan's ultimate tool to keep men in chains. But one Man changed all that. He died, but he didn't stay dead. He broke Satan's power when he tore off the bars of death. Now no one need fear death any longer. *Death still comes to all men, but for those who know Jesus (and only for them), death has changed its character.* It is no longer the entrance into the dim unknown. It is now the passageway into the presence of God.

What Happens When We Die?

There is one great lesson we should take away from this story of the final words of the Lord Jesus. Death holds no fear for the Christian, for when we die, we pass from this life into the hands of our heavenly Father, and he will take care of us.

What happens to believers when they die?

> 1. Our body is buried and our spirit goes to God.
> 2. We pass into the personal presence of God.
> 3. We pass from this life into paradise.
> 4. We are in the Father's hands.

These things are true for the followers of Jesus, because what happened to him will one day happen to them. Where he leads, they will one day follow.

"Our People Die Well"

John Wesley, the founder of Methodism, used to offer this comment as a final apologetic for the evangelical faith: "Our people die well." Those words sound odd and out of place in the twenty-first century. But several centuries ago it was popular to read books about the art of dying—how to face it with strength and grace. Dying well is one mark of a robust Christian faith. There is such a thing as "dying grace," which the Lord is pleased to give to his children.

We know that this life is incomplete. Even the best and most talented come to the end of life and look back with a sense of work undone, dreams unfulfilled, and gifts never developed. And we all have memories of foolish mistakes, things we wish we hadn't said or done, stupid decisions that hurt us and others, choices that led us down the wrong path, sometimes for years at a time. We all feel this way if we are honest. As I grow older and a bit wiser, I feel it more and more in my own heart. This world is not a safe place, nor is it a place where I can truly feel at home. There is a real sense in which we are born dying. *We come into the world saying hello, but almost immediately we start saying good-bye.* We grow up, graduate, leave home, move away, get married, have children, they grow up, graduate, leave home, move away, get married, have children who grow up—and the process continues. All the while we are saying good-bye. Such is life in a fading world. The psalmist said it well when he prayed, *"Show me, O Lord, my life's end and the number of my days; let me know how fleeting is my life. You have made my days a mere handbreadth; the span of my years is as nothing before you. Each man's life is but a breath"* (Ps. 39:4–5).

How many of us have completed some great project, achieved a great goal, fulfilled a long-cherished dream, finally checked off everything on our to-do list, only to find that we are still vaguely unhappy? We climbed to the top of the mountain, and when we got there, we discovered it wasn't worth the journey. And we said to ourselves, "Is that all there is?" Three thousand years ago Solomon put his finger on the problem when he declared that God has put eternity in the heart of every person (Eccl. 3:11). *We were made for God and we were made to know God. And we can't really be happy until we have a relationship with him.* That's the vast "God-shaped vacuum" inside every heart. We were created with a "homing instinct" for the God who made us. Heaven is our true home, and we will never be happy anywhere else.

That is why Paul was not afraid to die. *"Yes, we are fully confident, and we would rather be away from these bodies, for then we will be at home with the Lord"* (2 Cor. 5:8 NLT). That's a wonderful phrase—"at home with the Lord." If I ask where you go when your work is done, you'll probably say that you go home, referring to the place where you currently live. But at best that's only your temporary earthly home. Our true home is in heaven with the Lord Jesus Christ.

The Nursery of Eternity

What does it all mean for us? It certainly means that death is good news for the Christian. Right now we are like the caterpillar firmly stuck to the soil of planet earth. We can only dream of soaring to the heights. But in us there is a new nature calling us upward, to a new and better life. *Someday we'll crawl inside the cocoon called death and by God's grace we will emerge like butterflies, born to a new kind of life.* We don't look like butterflies now, but that's truly what we are meant to be. We were made to soar higher than the angels because we have been redeemed by the blood of Christ.

What, then, is this life? It is the nursery of eternity. We either use the sixty or seventy or eighty years we are given to improve our souls through the knowledge of Christ, or we waste these years in earthly pursuits and end up destitute and lost. *"For what profit is it to a man if he gains the whole world, and loses his own soul?"* (Matt. 16:26 NKJV). Thousands of years ago Job spoke for all of us when he asked, *"If a man dies, will he live again?"* (Job 14:14). The answer is yes. If you know Jesus, you live forever with him. But if you don't know Jesus, your future is grim indeed.

Death may seem to triumph for a season as it enters into our homes, and one by one, takes those nearest and dearest to us. Sooner or later death will come for you and for me, but death cannot win in the end. Jesus fought and won that battle two thousand years ago. There's an old gospel song called "Since Jesus Came into My Heart." One of the verses contains this phrase, "There's a light in the valley of death now for me, since

Jesus came into my heart." We still have to go through the valley of death, but it's not dark anymore. Jesus entered the valley for us, and he left the light on so we could find our way to heaven. The child of God need not fear death, for the grave has lost its victory. In the hour of death if you know Jesus, you may be sure that the grave is but a doorway to glory. Death will not win in the end. That's why Paul could say, "Where O death, is your victory? Where O death, is your sting?" (1 Cor. 15:55).

Years ago I heard Stanley Collins, then director of the Forest Home Conference Center in California, tell a story from his days with the British Army in World War II. One day he and another soldier came upon an unexploded land mine. Later that night he nearly passed out when he walked into the barracks and found his buddy resting his head on the same mine. Then he discovered that his buddy had removed the firing pin, rendering the land mine harmless. What had been an instrument of destruction had become a pillow for a weary soldier.

Jesus has taken the sting out of death and given us victory over the grave. For all the wonderful things that we have experienced at the hand of the Lord, we still must pass through the valley of the shadow of death. Our hope is this. That he who has seen us this far will not abandon us when we need him most. He will be with us when we must cross the dark Jordan. He will personally escort us to the mansions of eternal light.

Cheer up, child of God. Smile through your tears. Death is not the worst that can happen to us. The best is yet to come.

A Truth to Remember: Jesus died in accordance with God's plan, at precisely the right moment, in exactly the right way, accomplishing all that the Father intended from before the foundation of the world.

Going Deeper

1. Read Psalm 31. Circle or underline every verse that seems to refer to the circumstances surrounding the death of Christ.

2. Given that Jesus was tried, beaten, scourged, and crucified alongside two criminals, in what sense can we say that he was in control of all the circumstances surrounding his death?

3. When you think of your earthly father's hands, what images come to mind? What does the phrase "the Father's hands" suggest to you?

4. What does this final saying from the cross suggest about the importance of reading and memorizing Scripture? About teaching Scripture to your children? What steps are you taking in this area?

5. Make a list of the Old Testament prophecies that were fulfilled in the death of Jesus Christ.

6. In what ways is the death of Christ a model for how people of faith should approach their own death?

part 2

The Deeper Meaning of the Cross

Let us fix our eyes on Jesus, the author and perfecter of our
faith, who for the joy set before him endured the cross, scorning
its shame, and sat down at the right hand
of the throne of God.
HEBREWS 12:2

*"God presented him as a sacrifice of atonement,
through faith in his blood."*
ROMANS 3:25

chapter 8
where grace and wrath meet: what the cross meant to god

AT THIS POINT THERE IS NO NEED to repeat the details of what happened on Good Friday. Most of us know the story very well. We all understand that the cross is the very heart of the Christian faith, and without the cross we have no faith at all. What happened on that bloody hill was the single most important event in all history since the very beginning of the universe. No event can be compared to it. It is the dividing line of history and the key to understanding the message of the Bible.

It would be a good thing for all of us to see the cross in a new perspective and to ponder its deeper meaning. In order to do that we will look at the cross from seven distinct points of view in this chapter and the remainder of this book.

1. What the cross meant to God.
2. What it meant to Christ.
3. What it meant to Satan.
4. What it means to the world.
5. What it means to the church.
6. What it means to the Christian's struggle against sin.
7. What it means in heaven.

We begin by asking what happened on the cross from God's point of view. What did it mean to God the Father as his Son, the Lord Jesus Christ, died a criminal's death? In order to answer that question we will focus on just three verses—Romans 3:24–26. This passage has been called "the marrow of theology," and well it should be because it contains the heart and soul of the Christian gospel. These verses contain three answers to the question, What did the cross mean to God?

Answer #1: The Turning Away of God's Wrath

The NIV translates the first part of verse 25 this way: "*God presented him as a sacrifice of atonement, through faith in his blood.*" The phrase "sacrifice of atonement" translates a Greek word that means "propitiation." Few people have ever heard the word *propitiation,* and fewer still understand what it means. Here's a simple definition: *To turn away wrath by the offering of a gift.* In this context it means that the death of Christ turns away God's wrath.

I realize that God's wrath is not a popular topic these days. Many pastors fear to preach on God's wrath, lest they incur the wrath of the congregation. We'd all rather hear about God's love than about his wrath. Yet both are entirely biblical because both wrath and love flow from God's basic nature. While it is true that "God is love" (1 John 4:8), it is also true that he hates the wicked and those who do violence (Ps. 11:5). Sometimes in our attempt to appear compassionate, we proclaim that God "hates the sin and loves the sinner." I caution against using that statement indiscriminately because it is only partly true and can be misleading. Does God love sinners? Yes, he does because sinners are part of the world Christ came to save (John 3:16). But as it stands, the statement seems to imply that love is God's only response to sin. Check out the Book of Psalms and you will discover that God hates sinners and he abhors the wicked (Ps. 5:4–5; 37:13, 20; 101:7; 119:119). Much modern gospel preaching is anemic precisely because we preach less than the whole truth to guilty sinners. If all we say to the lost is "God loves you," we are in danger of making them think that their continued rebellion doesn't matter to God. Instead, we must warn them to flee from the wrath to come (Luke 3:7).[1]

And if we must say, "God hates sin but loves the sinner," let us at least add this phrase, "and he warns the sinner to repent before it is too late." When Jonathan Edwards preached his famous sermon "Sinners in the Hands of an Angry God," the listeners held on to the pillars of the building lest they suddenly slip down into eternal damnation. Can anyone imagine that happening today?

Lest I be misunderstood, let me say that I believe fervently in God's love. But God's love, as magnificent as it is, cannot cancel God's holy hatred of sin. There is no conflict between love and anger. True love is often angry. Ask any wife and she will say (at one time or another), "I'm angry because the one I love has disappointed me." Because God is holy, he is angry over our sin. Because he is love, he provided a means to turn away his own anger by the offering of his Son.

In pagan religions, the worshipers offer animal sacrifices to appease their gods. A pastor in Haiti told me that at least 90 percent of the Haitian people practice voodoo to one degree or another. Sometimes they will slaughter a chicken and place the blood (with the entrails) on a dish by the front door, hoping to ward off evil spirits. It is their way of appeasing the god who stands behind voodoo. That is the pagan idea of propitiation.

On a completely different level, we see propitiation at work when a husband realizes that he has offended his wife. Hoping to make it up to her, he stops on the way home and buys flowers and candy and a card. Before she can say a word, he gives her the gifts, hoping to turn away her wrath and restore a good relationship.

But the greatest illustration comes from the Old Testament Day of Atonement (Yom Kippur) when the high priest would enter the Holy of Holies with the blood of a goat. Leviticus 16 describes the ritual in exacting detail. It must be the high priest and he alone, and it must happen on the Day of Atonement—and on no other day. On the Day of Atonement the high priest would take off his regular clothes and put on a sacred linen tunic. He would sprinkle the goat blood on the lid of the Ark of the Covenant. That lid—made of beaten gold—was called the "Mercy Seat." Inside the Ark was a copy of the Ten Commandments—representing the Law of God. By the sprinkling of the blood, the sins of the people were "covered." That covering by means of blood was called the "atonement." The sacrifice of blood turned away the wrath of God. Why is this important? Because God's justice demands death as the ultimate punishment for sin.

A Friendly Father, Not an Angry God

What does the symbolism of the Day of Atonement represent? During the other days of the year when God looked down from heaven, he saw the Ten Commandments inside the Ark. The Ten Commandments stood as a testimony against the sins of the nation of Israel. But on the Day of Atonement God saw the blood of the sacrifice that covered the sin of the people of Israel.

The sacrificial system had one major problem. It provided temporary forgiveness because it was based on the blood of animals. We know that "it is impossible for the blood of bulls and goats to take away sins" (Heb. 10:4). That is why every year, year after year, the high priest would go in and do it all over again. And when he died, another high priest would take his place and do the same thing each year on the Day of Atonement. The Old Testament system provided no permanent forgiveness for sin (Heb. 7:23–28).

When Jesus died on the cross, the blood that he shed was like the blood on the Mercy Seat. It turned away the wrath of God and covered the sin of the entire human race. How could that be? In the Old Testament it is the blood of bulls and goats; in the New Testament it is the blood of Jesus Christ that has eternal value in the eyes of God. When Jesus hung on the cross, he cried out, "My God, my God, why have you forsaken me?" (Mark 15:34). In that moment all the wrath of God was poured out on Jesus. He became sin for us, and all of your sin and all of mine and the sins of the whole world were poured out on Jesus. In that moment God turned his face away from his own Son. To call the death of Christ a "propitiation" means that God's wounded heart is now satisfied with the death of his Son. When a sinner trusts Christ, God accepts him on the basis of the bloody sacrifice Christ made when he died on the cross.

Why did God do it this way? Because he is an infinite God of infinite holiness, all sins committed against him are infinite in magnitude. Only a gift of infinite value could turn away the infinite wrath of God. And only God himself (in the Person of his Son) could make such an infinite gift. That's why our piddling efforts to turn aside God's wrath are doomed to failure. We think that going to church or being baptized or going to Mass or saying our prayers or being good or stopping a bad habit or "trying hard to be better" will somehow turn away the infinite wrath of God. The wonder of propitiation is that the offended party (God), who has every right to be angry at sinners himself, offers the gift (the death of Christ) to turn away his own wrath, thus making it possible for guilty sinners to be forgiven.

Therefore, when we come to God through Christ, we come to a friendly Father and not to an angry God.

Answer #2: A Demonstration of God's Justice

In verse 25 and again in verse 26 Paul says that God set forth Christ as a propitiation for sin *"to demonstrate his justice"* so that he might be *"just and the one who justifies those who have faith in Jesus"* (v. 26). While serving as a guest host on a national call-in program, I received a call from a man in Miami who asked why Christ had to die on the cross for our sins. He seemed troubled by this fact and said that he didn't believe that Christ had died in our place, standing in our stead, as a substitute, taking our punishment. I tried to answer his question by referring to Romans 3:25–26. What the listeners didn't know is that while I was answering the question, he was shouting into the phone. We had taken him off the air, but evidently he didn't realize it or didn't care. The very notion of Christ as our substitute seemed to anger him greatly.

He's not the only one who feels this way. Several years ago Phil Donahue, who hosted a popular TV talk show for many years, listed the various reasons why he had become disillusioned with Christianity. Among them was this: "How could an all-knowing, all-loving God allow his Son to be murdered on a cross to redeem my sins?" That's an excellent question because it goes to the very heart of the gospel.[2]

Why did Jesus have to die? Why would God put his own Son to death, especially to save people who had rebelled against him? In searching for the answer, it helps to think of another question: Since God is both all-powerful and infinitely gracious, why didn't he simply offer forgiveness to anyone who says, "I'm sorry"? Many people secretly think that's what God should have done. Then we wouldn't have to deal with the embarrassment of God killing his own Son.

Sin Must Be Punished

The answer goes like this. From a human point of view, God had a problem. Because God is holy, he cannot allow sin to go unpunished. His justice demands that every sin be punished—no matter how small it may seem to us. If he were to forgive sin without proper punishment, he would cease to be holy and just. God would no longer be God because he would have denied his own character. That could not happen. All offenses against God must be punished. That's why sinners can't simply say, "I'm sorry" and instantly be forgiven. Someone has to pay the price.

We follow this same principle in our criminal justice system. Suppose a man is found guilty of embezzling six million dollars from his employer. Let us further suppose that just before sentencing, he stands before the judge, confesses his crime, begs for mercy, and promises never to embezzle money again. How would you react if the judge accepted his apology and released him with no punishment? Suppose the man had been convicted of rape and then was set free with no punishment simply because he apologized. Or what if he apologized for murdering a father and a mother in front of their children—and the judge set him free? Let us go further and ask about a group of terrorists who break into the White House and murder the president. Upon their capture, trial, and conviction, they apologize and promise never to murder a president again, and are released on a promise of good behavior. What would we do with the judge who set them free? We would throw that judge in jail for a long time.[3]

Even in this life a price must be paid for breaking the law. When lawbreakers are set free with no punishment, respect for the law disappears. When assassins are not punished, respect for the presidency disappears. The same principle applies to raising children. When parents refuse to discipline with tough love, they sometimes end up raising criminals instead of responsible adults. The same is true in the spiritual realm. When sin is not punished, it doesn't seem very sinful. God's "problem" was to devise a plan of salvation whereby he would remain holy and just, and still provide a way of forgiveness for guilty sinners. Somewhere, somehow, there had to be a place where grace and wrath could meet. That place is the cross of Christ.

Back to Phil Donahue for a moment. He asked a second question that deserves an answer: "If God the Father is so 'all-loving,' why didn't He come down and go to Calvary?" The answer is, he did. He did! God came down to this earth in the Person of his Son, the Lord Jesus Christ, and died for our sins.

The paradox of salvation is this: God is a God of love . . . and therefore wants to forgive sinners. But he is also a God of holiness . . . who must not and cannot overlook sin. How could God love sinners and yet not overlook their sin? No one would ever have dreamed of his answer. God sent his own Son to die for sinners. In that way, the just punishment for sin was fully met in the death of Christ, and sinners who trust in Christ could be freely forgiven. Only God could have done something like that. Thus, Paul says, God is both just (in punishing sin) and the justifier of those who believe in Jesus.

Think of it. In the death of this one Man, all the sins of the human race are fully paid for—past, present, and future. *As a result, those who believe in Jesus find that their sins are gone forever.* This is the heart of the gospel: God's holiness demands that sin be punished. God's grace provides the sacrifice. *What God demands, he supplies.* Thus salvation is a work of God from first to last. It is *conceived* by God, *provided* by God, and *applied* by God.

Answer #3: An Outpouring of God's Grace

Romans 3:24 tells us that we "are justified *freely* by his grace." The word *freely* literally means "without a cause." Salvation comes "without a cause" in us. That is, God saves us in spite of the fact that he can't find a reason within us to save us. Salvation is a "free gift" to the human race. There is nothing in us that causes God to want to save us. No good works, no inner beauty, no great moral attainment, no intellectual merit of any kind. When God saves us, he does it in spite of the fact that we don't deserve it.

Not long ago I ran across an excellent definition of grace: *What you need but do not deserve.* God declares us righteous when we have nothing but the sewage of sin in our veins. This is the doctrine of free grace. God saves people who don't deserve it. God saves people who actually deserve condemnation. God saves people in spite of themselves and contrary to their record. It is "pure, abounding, astounding grace!"

Let me go a step further. When God saves people, he doesn't do it because of any potential he sees in them. I think most of us secretly feel (though we would never say it) that there must have been something in us worth saving. Human pride dies hard. But it's not as if God saw a musician and said, "We need a good piano player in the church. I think I'll save him." Or, "She's got a lot of money and we could use some extra cash for world missions." Or, "Those twins would make excellent ushers. I want them on my team." No, no, a thousand times no. God doesn't save on the basis of your potential. Apart from the grace of God, the only potential you have is the potential for eternal damnation.

Jesus Stood in My Shoes

When God saves, he saves us by free grace, wholly apart from anything in us or anything we might "bring to the table" later. This is a shocking truth, hard to hear, but entirely biblical. And in the end, it is most comforting because it means that anyone, anywhere, at any time can come to Christ for salvation. No one has any advantage since "there is no difference" because "all have sinned and fall short of the glory of God" (Rom. 3:23).

The story is told about an elderly country woman named Betty who trusted in Christ for salvation. One of her skeptical friends heard about it, and intending to make fun of her, asked if she had indeed become one of the saints. "Yes, I have," she replied. "Well," said the skeptic, "are you now an expert in theology?" "I'm no Bible scholar," Betty replied. "I'm simply positive that

God loves me enough that he'd rather go to hell than have me go there, and that God loves me enough that he'd rather leave heaven and die than for me not to get to heaven to be with him." The skeptic insisted, "Is that all you know about it? Can't you at least explain what being saved by grace means—that is one of your central doctrines, isn't it?" Betty thought for a moment, then answered with these words: "Jesus stood in my shoes at Calvary; now I'm standing in his." It would be hard to find a better explanation of justification by grace.[4]

This is so hard for us to believe. We would prefer to work for our salvation. But God's gift of salvation costs us nothing, even though it cost Christ everything. The Lord now says to us, "Take it by faith! It's yours for free. I have paid the cost for you."

Has the blood of Jesus ever been applied to your heart? God's Son has made propitiation. He has turned away the wrath of God. He shed his blood, and what was a place of judgment is now a mercy seat for anyone and everyone who will come to God through Jesus Christ.

A friend told me about a billboard posted near a Chicago freeway advertising the cardiac services of Christ Hospital in the Oak Lawn area. The billboard reads: "Christ is #1 in Open Heart Surgeries." I don't know about the hospital, but I can vouch for its namesake. Jesus Christ is indeed #1 in open-heart surgery. He has never lost a case yet. When you come to him by faith, he gives you a brand-new heart.

Because of the cross, salvation is now entirely free. What then must I do to be saved? Must I be holy? Must I be good? Must I change my ways? Must I promise to clean up my act? Here is God's answer: Romans 3:24 says, "Freely by his grace." But the human heart cries out, "I must do something. I must make my contribution." So we clean up our act, we go to church, we pay our money, we go to Mass, we enter the waters of baptism, and on and on. We think God will never forgive us until we do something to deserve it. But it is not so. God gives his justification away freely and if you try to pay for it, he will throw it in your face.

Don't Wait to Get Better

If I said you can be justified for $5, who would not pay? If I said you must walk a hundred miles, we'd all line up tomorrow morning. If I said God will justify you if you will endure a twenty-minute beating, would we not endure the pain and count it a small cost? But if I say, "Free, free, God's grace is free," something in the human heart rebels against that fact. Either you take it freely, or you don't take it at all.[5]

How then do we receive God's gift of salvation? *Simply by asking for it.* Do you know in your heart that you want Christ in your life? You may have him today. This is the wonder of the gospel. Do not say, "I'll do my best and come to Christ later." That is the language of hell. You cannot be saved as long as you hold to your notions of goodness.

"I'll get better," you say. No you won't. You can't get better; that's your problem. You're as good as you can be right now—and that's not very good. Sin has gripped your soul and made you depraved inside and out. Here's some shocking news. If you somehow got better, you would be worse off, because the worse you are, the better it is to come to Christ (Luke 5:32). If you are unholy and you know it, come to Christ. If you are a sinner and wish to be forgiven, come to Christ. If you feel unworthy, come to Christ. If you feel like a failure, come to Christ. If you admit that your life is a mess, come to Christ.

You must run to the cross as your only hope of salvation. God is fully satisfied with the work of his Son. The demands of the Law have been fully met. Grace and wrath have met at the cross and the result is the free offer of salvation to everyone who believes. If you have any stirring in your heart, any sense of your need, any desire to be saved by grace, that desire has been placed in your heart by God. May that desire lead you to the cross where Jesus waits to receive you.

Going Deeper

A Truth to Remember: *When we come to God through Christ, we come to a friendly Father, not to an angry God.*

1. Read Leviticus 16. Make a list of the various events that took place on the Day of Atonement. Which ones seem to clearly picture the sacrifice of Christ on the cross for our sins?

2. Why do you think some people are offended by the notion of Christ dying in our place, for our sins, bearing our penalty, to turn away the wrath of God?

3. "God loves the sinner and hates the sin." Is this an adequate statement? How would you change it to make it more biblical?

4. Using the material in this chapter, summarize God's "problem" in finding a way to forgive sin while still upholding the principle of divine justice.

5. "God saves us in spite of the fact that he can't find a reason within us to save us." Do you agree? Explain what is meant by the phrase "free grace."

6. Why is it dangerous and wrong for a person to say, "I'll come to Christ after I've cleaned up my life?"

"God made him who had no sin to be sin for us, so that in him we might become the righteousness of God."
2 CORINTHIANS 5:21

chapter 9

He Became sin for us: what the cross meant to christ

THIS IS ONE OF THE MOST magnificent verses in all the Bible. Spurgeon called it the heart of the gospel. It is the gospel in one verse. Everything you need to know about how to go to heaven can be found in these twenty-three words. There is an amazing simplicity here— twenty-one words of only one syllable, one word of two syllables, and one word (righteousness) of three syllables. It could hardly be simpler than this—yet whole books could be written on the meaning of each phrase.[1]

How important is this verse? Miss this, and you've missed the truth of God. If you get this right, you can be wrong in a lot of other places and still go to heaven. In these days of rampant theological confusion, it is vitally important that the church of Jesus Christ be firmly settled on the gospel message. That is, after all, our only message. God has not committed to us a message about political power or military might. We are not called to right all the wrongs in the world or to pass judgment on every passing trend. The church has been given one major task—to preach the gospel to every person on earth (Mark 16:15).

If that is our God-given task, then it behooves us to make sure we know what the gospel is. And we shouldn't take for granted that all church members (much less all Christians) truly know the gospel. Our problem is twofold. First, we have drifted into believing that "God helps those who help themselves," which may be popular but has nothing to do with true biblical salvation. Second, we have heard the gospel so many times that it no longer amazes us. Perhaps you recall that the famous *Star Wars* movie trilogy was rereleased several years ago with additional computer-generated footage that was not included in the original version. It was advertised with this slogan: "*Star Wars:* See it again for the first time." I hope something like that happens as we consider the deeper meaning of the cross of Christ—that we will "see it again for the first time."[2]

Second Corinthians 5:21 tells us what the cross meant to *Christ.* Each phrase tells of a miracle that cannot be fully explained but must be accepted by faith. Let's begin by considering the character of the one who was crucified.

His Character: He Had No Sin

Paul begins with the fact that Christ "had no sin." Some versions say that he "knew no sin," stressing the sinless nature of his inner being. There was no sin outwardly because there was no sin inwardly. When Jesus Christ walked on the earth, he was perfectly righteous. Stated negatively, he was without fault, without sin, and without evil. He never did anything wrong, never broke any laws of God, and never deviated in the slightest degree from the path of God's will.

This is crucial because if Christ had sinned, he could not be our Savior. A sinner could not pay for the sins of another sinner. The sacrifice must be made by one who was without spot or blemish—like the lambs slain on the night of the final plague in Egypt (Exod. 12). God ordained that the lambs must be one-year-old males, in good health, free from disease and physical defect. The lambs that were slaughtered in Egypt pictured the coming "Lamb of God" who by his bloody, sacrificial death would take away the sin of the world (John 1:29 KJV).

How do we know that Christ had no sin? Primarily from the testimony of his adversaries. When the Roman governor Pontius Pilate examined him, he declared, *"I find no fault in him"* (John 19:4 KJV). When Herod and the Jewish leaders put him on trial, they could find no witnesses against him so they rounded up false witnesses who lied under oath (Matt. 26:59–60). When Christ hung on the cross, the Roman centurion cried out, *"Truly this was the Son of God"* (Matt. 27:54 KJV).

He knew all about sin, but he never sinned—not even once. He lived in a sinful world, but the stain of sin never tarnished his character. Of all the billions of people who have lived on planet earth, he is the only one about whom it can be truly said that he never sinned in word, in thought, or in deed. There is no hint of moral contamination surrounding his name. He faced temptation head-on, full strength, all that the devil could throw at him, but having felt its full weight, he never gave in, never flinched, never even came close to sinning. He never confessed a fault because he had no faults to confess. He never asked for a pardon because he never needed one. He claimed that no one could convict him of sin (John 8:46), and he was right. To use an old term that is precisely accurate, Christ was and is a "moral miracle."[3] That is why the writer of Hebrews could say that he was tempted in all points as we are, yet he was without sin (Heb. 4:15).

His Sacrifice: He Became Sin for Us

Here is the second miracle of our text. Jesus the sinless Son of God became sin for us. How could this be? Some translations attempt to soften the blow by translating "sin offering" instead of "sin." Although that is acceptable in terms of the Greek language, it is not necessary. Paul is not suggesting that Christ literally became a sinner. Such a thing would be not possible. Christ remained personally sinless while hanging on the cross. He never committed a sin and therefore never became a sinner. However, in some sense that is beyond our understanding he "became sin" for us. Perhaps the best way to understand this is to say that God treated his Son as if he were a sinner. He so identified with sinners that he "was numbered with the transgressors" (Isa. 53:12). He not only died between two sinners; he was numbered with them and died as they died—a criminal's death on the cross.

Historically Christians have used two phrases to describe how Christ "became sin" for us.

He Took Our Place—"For Us"

When Christ died on the cross, he took my place—and he took yours. *This is the doctrine of substitution*—that Christ died in the place of guilty sinners. Think of it this way. His nails were meant for you, the crown of thorns should have been on your head, the spear should have pierced your side, and the jeers and insults were meant for you. It should have been you hanging on a tree—but it wasn't. It was Jesus dying in your place.

Having said that, we must quickly add that this has been a controversial doctrine across the centuries. Not everyone believes it is true. Some have mocked the doctrine of substitutionary atonement, saying that it is a holdover from the primitive pagan religions of the ancient world. Some have derided it as a "slaughterhouse religion." Years ago some Protestant denominations removed all the hymns that mentioned the blood of Christ from their hymnbooks because they were embarrassing to modern men and women. Be that as it may. True biblical religion is an offense to the natural mind. The world by wisdom did not know God (1 Cor. 1:21) and has always stumbled over the cross. The death of Jesus offends the sensibilities of those who want a cultured, bloodless religion. I don't have the time to refute that notion except to say that the Bible is a book of blood from beginning to end. Take out the blood and you have taken out God's plan of salvation. "Without the shedding of blood there is no forgiveness of sin" (Heb. 9:22).

You cannot avoid the doctrine of substitution because this is the teaching of the New Testament. It is not just that men treated him so badly; it is that God ordained his death on the cross. When he died, he died taking the place of the very people who put him to death.

He Took Our Penalty—"He Became Sin"

This follows from the first truth. On the cross Jesus became the sinless Sin-Bearer. He paid the price we owed to God, the debt we could never pay. His death satisfied God's righteous decree that sin must always be punished.

In the last chapter I mentioned the blood of the goat that the high priest sprinkled on the Mercy Seat in the Holy of Holies on the Day of Atonement (see Lev. 16 for details). The sprinkled blood signified the covering of the sins of the people for one more year. Did you know that two goats were involved on the Day of Atonement? One was killed and the other was not. After the priest offered the blood of the first goat, he then placed his hands on the head of the second goat, confessing the sins of the people. Leviticus 16:21 specifically says he is to "put them" (the sins of the people) on the goat. Then the goat was taken into the wilderness and released. This pictured the removal of sin by placing it on an innocent victim. That goat was called the scape-goat because he symbolically took the sins of the people on himself (Lev. 16:20–22). What the goat did symbolically, Jesus did literally. He removed our sins from us *"as far as the east is from the west"* (Ps. 103:12).

Isaiah 53:6 says that *"the Lord has laid on him* (that is, on Christ) *the iniquity of us all."* Let's suppose that all your sins have been written in one massive book. That book is heavy because it records every rotten thing you've ever said, every unkind word you've ever spoken, every mean thought, every lustful fantasy, every evil imagination, and all your bad attitudes from the day of your birth till the day of your death. Picture yourself trying to hold that massive book in your hands. Now picture Jesus stand-ing next to you. He is holy, perfect, pure, and good. He has no book in his hands because he has never sinned. You want to be rid of the book, but you can't seem to find a place to put it down. What will you do? Now picture Christ on the cross, with the weight of millions of books upon his bleeding back. He bears that crushing weight as long as he can, then he dies. Look closely and you will see that each book is the personal record of someone who lived on the earth. If you look closely, you can see your book too. He took your sins—the record of all your evil and all your failings and all your shortcomings—he took it all upon himself when he died on the cross. Truly, the Lord laid on him the iniquity of us all.

We will never understand this. If someone says, "It doesn't make sense," I heartily agree. From the world's point of view, we cannot fathom how one man could die in the place of another, bearing his penalty, and thus providing him a right standing with God. We can imagine human illustrations of one man dying for another's benefit, but the benefit ends with this life. We cannot conceive how a death in time could provide eternal benefits. Yet that is precisely what the Bible teaches. The issue is not does it make sense? The issue is whether it is true and do you believe it?[4]

We do not worry about what the world says or what it thinks. The world does not know God and cannot know him apart from divine revelation. This is what we know—that Christ died for the sins of the world and that in his death God himself has suffered on our behalf. We believe that God in Christ made himself sin for man, and that man in Christ is now made the righteousness of God. This is a true miracle, and like all miracles cannot be explained but it cannot be refuted either. It can only be believed or denied.

Ponder these two truths from the sacrifice of Christ: (1) Sin must be exceedingly sinful. (2) God's grace is beyond all comprehension. How much God must love us to do something like this!

His Gift: We Might Become the Righteousness of God

We come to the third and final miracle in this verse—that in him we become the righteousness of God. This is what we all want—to be made right with God, to have our record cleared, to know that when we go to sleep at night there is nothing between us and our heavenly Father.

In this final phrase we have the Great Exchange:

He was condemned that we might be justified.

He bore our sin that we might be set free.

He died that we might live.

He suffered that we might be redeemed.

He was made sin that we might be made righteous.

Theologians have a term for this exchange. *They call it the doctrine of imputation.* This term from the banking world means that when we trust Christ, our sin is credited to his account and his righteousness is credited to our account. He takes our debt, and we get his credit. He paid what we owed (and could never pay) and he gives us what he has (and we could never earn).

Some people say this is impossible. Skeptics call this a legal fiction. How can the righteousness of one man be given to another? On earth I cannot literally take your sin, and you cannot literally take my righteousness. The answer to the dilemma is profoundly simple: With man this is impossible; with God all things are possible. "I cannot accept it," you say. Then you will never be saved. There is no salvation apart from this because receiving his righteousness by faith is what salvation is all about. It's not as if God has a Plan B for people who don't like Plan A. You come to God by way of the cross or you don't come at all.

The Four Turnabouts

Dr. Lewis Sperry Chafer, the founder of Dallas Theological Seminary, illustrated God's attitude toward sinners this way. His illustration is called "The Four Turnabouts." First, he took his hands and placed them together with palms touching each other. That pictures God and Adam and Eve in perfect harmony with God in the Garden of Eden before the Fall. Then he took his right hand and turned it so that the palm faced outward and away from the left hand. That pictures Adam and Eve turning from God after the Fall. Then he took his left hand and faced it outward away from his right hand. This pictures God judging Adam and Even (and the whole human race) by casting them out of the Garden. Now both hands are facing away from each other. Finally, he took his left hand and brought it slowly back around so that the palm faced inward—in its original position. This pictures God having been reconciled by the cross of Christ (2 Cor. 5:18–20). Even though the right hand is still facing outward and away from the left, the left hand now faces toward the right—just as God faces the sinner and begs him to be reconciled. "Won't you come home?" God calls out to the guilty sinner. That is God's word to the world—be reconciled to God![5]

Let me say it as plainly as I can. There is nothing except your sin that stands between you and God. God's wrath was turned away in the death of his Son; his justice has been satisfied, his love poured out to the world. Now you must choose—your sins or Jesus Christ! Damnation or salvation! If you come to God through Christ, you will be accepted. You will not, you cannot, be turned away.

"Can I Be a Christian?"

An international student (from Japan, I believe) who had been attending the church I pastor wrote to ask me a very important question:

Dear Dr. Ray Pritchard,

I have come to your church about two months,
and I like [it] there a lot. I began to read the Bible
by myself, and I want to be a Christian. However, I
don't know how I can be a Christian. I want to talk
to you about it, but I am a little shy, so I write to
you. Can I be a Christian? Would you tell me how
I am able to be a Christian? I am looking forward
to hearing from you. Thank you very much. (I'm
sorry, my writing is not too good.)

How do you answer a letter like that? Even though she was
just learning English, you can sense the deep desire of her heart
coming through those simple words. Here is part of what I wrote
her:

You asked, "Can I be a Christian?" The answer is
yes. You can be a Christian. The most important
thing I can say to you is that being a Christian
means having a personal relationship with Jesus
Christ.

In order to have a personal relationship with
Jesus Christ, you must trust him as your Savior.
Does that sound strange? I hope not. Already you
know much about Jesus. You know that he worked
many miracles and helped many people. But the
most important thing to know about Jesus is that
he died on the cross for your sins. That is, when he
died on the cross two thousand years ago, he took
your place. You should have died there. But he died
in your place, as your substitute, and by his death
he paid the price for all your sins.

That's a lot to think about, and you don't have to fully understand it (no one fully understands it), but you do have to believe it. That's what trusting is. It's believing, really believing in your heart that something is true. Trusting is what you do when you get on an airplane. You trust your life to the fact that the airplane will safely take you up in the air and then safely get you back to the ground again. That's trust. It's staking your life upon something you believe to be true.

Trusting Jesus Christ means staking your life upon the fact that when he died on the cross, he really did pay the price for your sins, and he really did take your place. So, do you believe that Jesus Christ died for you? Are you willing to stake your life upon that fact? If you are ready to say yes, then you can be a Christian.

Let me give you a simple prayer to pray. This prayer is not magic. You should only pray it if it expresses the real desire of your heart. But if it does, then you can pray this prayer:

Dear Lord Jesus,

Thank you for dying on the cross for me. Thank you for taking all my sin away. I believe you are the Son of God and the Savior of the world. I gladly take you as my Savior. Come into my life and make me a Christian. Please help me to live a life that will be pleasing to you. Thank you for hearing this prayer.

Amen.

That's simple, isn't it? If you will pray that
prayer and mean it from your heart, you can
become a Christian right now. I hope you will just
stop right now and pray that prayer to God.

Did you pray that prayer? I hope so. If you did, I
would be honored if you would tell me so. On
Sunday, if you do not feel too shy about it, you can
just come up to me and say, "Pastor Ray, I prayed
that prayer." I would be so happy if you would do
that.

I put the letter in the mail and wondered how my new friend
would receive it. Would it make sense? Would she understand it?

The very next Sunday she came up to me after the second
service and said with a shy smile that she had gotten my letter. I
asked her if she had read it. She said yes. I asked her if she had
prayed the prayer. She said yes. I asked if she understood what
the prayer meant. She said yes. I asked if the prayer expressed the
desire of her heart. She said yes.

Then I said, "Welcome. You are now a Christian." "That's all
I have to do to be a Christian?" she replied. When I said, "Yes,"
the most beautiful smile I have ever seen spread across her face
from one side to the other.

That is the power of faith when it is directed toward the
right object—Jesus Christ. Sometimes we forget how powerful
the gospel is and how easy it is for a sinner to be saved. I have
been preaching for thirty years, and I can say with conviction
that I have never known a sinner whom Christ would not
receive. I know thousands of people who have experienced the
life-transforming power of a personal relationship with Jesus
Christ.

What did the cross mean to Jesus Christ? He voluntarily took our sin that through faith in him we might become the right-eousness of God. He took our place and bore the penalty of our sin so that we might be set free and be fully accepted by God.

A Truth to Remember: *This is what we know—that Christ died for the sins of the world and that in his death God himself has suffered on our behalf.*

Going Deeper

1. Why is it important that Jesus Christ "knew no sin?" What happens when this truth is denied or minimized?

2. Read Exodus 12, the story of the Passover. How does the preparation of the Passover lamb foreshadow the death of Christ?

3. "The Bible is a book of blood from beginning to end." List as many examples as you can find that demonstrate this truth.

4. Did Jesus actually become a sinner while he was on the cross? What does the phrase "he became sin for us" mean?

5. "There is nothing except your sin that stands between and God." Do you agree? What sin in your life is sta   ng between you and God right now?

6. Practice "The Four Turnabouts" mentioned in thi napter. Share this illustration with a Christian friend. Then   God to give you a chance to share it with someone who c sn't know Christ personally.

"And having disarmed the powers and authorities, he made a public spectacle of them, triumphing over them by the cross."
COLOSSIANS 2:15

chapter 10

"one little word shall fell him": what the cross meant to satan

By 6:00 P.M. THE PARTY HAD started in earnest. It was Friday evening and that meant the party would probably last all night and perhaps even into the next day. Everyone who heard the news could hardly believe it, but they knew that if it were true, this would be the party to end all parties. So they came one by one, then in groups of five or ten, finally a crowd so large no one could begin to count them all.

It was the usual Friday night madness, with loud music, raucous laughter, off-color jokes, and plenty of booze for those who wanted to indulge, which was practically everyone. From time to time their host rose to make a speech to the cheers of the teeming throngs. He exuded the calm confidence of a man who has won his greatest victory. It was hard fought to be sure, and until the last moment he was nervous, but then it happened, and when it did, he knew he was the victor at last.

Hours passed and the music grew louder. They danced and sang and drank and cheered and laughed the night away. By Saturday morning, when you would have expected the crowd to thin, it actually grew larger—and louder—and even more raucous. If anyone had gone home, his place was taken by ten other happy revelers. And their host graciously stayed and partied with them. By Saturday night people from distant realms had joined them, making for an even merrier celebration. A few speeches were given, followed by one toast after another. Then more dancing, and in the darker corners, wild behavior.

Then it happened. No one knows the precise moment, but in the early hours on Sunday morning a messenger arrived and whispered something in the ear of the host, who seemed to grow faint at the news. Recovering quickly, he ordered several of his top men to check it out. A nervous murmur fell over the crowd. Within a few minutes the news had been confirmed.

Just that fast it happened. The music stopped, the dancing ended, and on Sunday morning the party in hell was over.

The scene is entirely imaginary, but the truth is very real. Hell's rejoicing was short-lived. *The party that started on Good Friday ended on Easter Sunday.* What seemed like Satan's greatest victory turned into his decisive defeat. How did it happen? What did the cross mean to Satan? A survey of the biblical evidence suggests six answers to that question.

Crushing the Serpent's Head

When Christ died on the cross, Satan's head was crushed. "And I will put enmity between you and the woman, and between your offspring and hers; he will crush your head, and you will strike his heel" (Gen. 3:15). This is the first promise given after Adam and Eve ate the forbidden fruit in the Garden of Eden. It is also the first gospel sermon ever preached. Theologians call it the *protoevangelium*—or "first gospel." These words spoken by God contain the first promise of redemption in the Bible. Everything else in the Bible flows from these words in Genesis 3:15. As the acorn contains the mighty oak, so these words contain the entire plan of salvation. The English preacher Charles Simeon called this verse "the sum and summary of the whole Bible."[1] Although you may not see it at first glance, Christ is in this verse. He is the ultimate Seed of the woman who would one day crush the serpent's ugly head. In the process his "heel" would be bruised on the cross. In short, this verse predicts that Jesus would win the victory over Satan but would himself be wounded at the same time. When Christ died on the cross, Satan struck his heel. Where on his body were the nails pounded in? His hands and his feet—right through his heels. On Friday about sundown, when they took the dead body of Jesus down from the cross, it appeared that Satan had won the battle. On Sunday morning, the true Victor walked out of the grave, alive from the dead.

Listen to these colorful words of Spurgeon:

> Look at your Master and your King upon the
> cross, all distained with blood and dust! There was
> his heel most cruelly bruised. When they take
> down that precious body and wrap it in fair white
> linen and in spices, and lay it in Joseph's tomb,
> they weep as they handle the casket in which the

Deity had dwelt, for there again Satan had bruised
his heel . . . . The devil had let loose Herod, and
Pilate, and Caiaphas, and the Jews, and the
Romans . . . . That is all, however! It is only his
heel, and not his head, that is bruised! For lo, the
Champion rises again![2]

Satan delivered a terrible blow to Jesus on Good Friday. No
doubt he thought he had thrown a knockout punch. But he was
wrong. All he did was strike Jesus on the heel. As painful as it was,
that suffering was nothing compared to what Jesus did to Satan.
"Satan has bruised the heel of Christ, but Christ has fetched him
such a blow on the head that he will never get over it."[3]

Destroying the Works of the Devil

When Christ died, he destroyed the works of the devil. First John
3:8b says that "the reason the Son of God appeared was to
destroy the devil's work." The word *destroy* doesn't mean to anni-
hilate; it means to "render powerless." When Jesus died on the
cross, he "pulled the plug" on Satan. In this present age Satan
seems to be very powerful, but he can do nothing without God's
express permission. He is like Samson shorn of his locks, unable
to do anything on his own. The day is coming when his utter
impotence will be revealed to the universe and those who followed him will discover that they were following a toothless
lion.

"Death Stinks"

When Christ died, Satan's power of death was broken forever.
Hebrews 2:14–15 expresses this in beautiful language, "*Since the
children have flesh and blood, he too shared in their humanity so that
by his death he might destroy him who holds the power of death—that*

is, the devil—and free those who all their lives were held in slavery by their fear of death." Down deep in the human heart there is a fear of death that Satan uses to keep us enslaved. Don't mistake the point. Satan has no power to kill you or anyone else. He can do nothing without God's permission. But he plays upon our fear of death to keep us in the chains of sin. That's why the Bible says "the sting of death is sin" (1 Cor. 15:56). When the unsaved die, they die with their sins still upon them, like a heavy burden, a vast weight bearing them down to hell. They die miserable, angry, frustrated, and fearful because they don't know what to do with their sins.

What a difference it makes to die having your sins forgiven! How many times have I heard Christians say when a loved one dies, "What do people do who don't know the Lord?" Death is hard enough to face if you are a Christian, but it is intolerable without the Lord. And yet every day countless thousands march into eternity with the leaden weight of sin hanging around their necks.

A friend who had seen a loved one die recently said it succinctly in just two words: "Death stinks." Yes, it does, which is why the Bible says that death is the last enemy that shall be destroyed (1 Cor. 15:26). Some people claim that death is a "natural" part of life. This is certainly true in the sense that death comes to all of us because this is a fallen world. Where sin exists, death is indeed "natural." But that is only part of the biblical picture. Death reigns because of Adam's sin (Rom. 5:12–14). But now through Jesus Christ we have his infallible Word that *"whoever lives and believes in me will never die"* (John 11:26). Like most pastors, I have quoted those verses often during funeral services. I like to do it when the dead person is in the casket right in front of me. After all, that's when the full impact of Jesus' words really hits home. Do we believe Jesus or not? John Stott comments that for the Christian, death has become a "trivial episode," a minor inconvenience and nothing more.[4] If we know Jesus, death is like closing our eyes and one moment later opening them in heaven.

Unbelievers don't have that privilege, nor do they understand our confidence as we enter death's door. For them death is the end—or so they think. For us it is the next step in our eternal life with God.

The Harrowing of Hell

When Christ died, the devil's prisoners were released. Luke 4:18 tells us Christ came to set the captives free and "to release the oppressed." Who are the captives Christ came to set free? We have already seen that the lost are enslaved to the devil through their fear of death. Christ came to open for us those prison doors and set the captives free.

It is possible that there may be even more to this. In chapter 2, I noted that when Jesus said, "Today you will be with me in paradise" (Luke 23:43), it indicates that he went to heaven between his crucifixion and the resurrection. I believe that is true, but it does not exhaust all the possibilities. In his book *I Believe in Satan's Downfall*, Michael Green speaks of the ancient doctrine called the "Harrowing of Hell." In the early church many people believed that between his crucifixion and resurrection, Christ went to the regions of darkness and proclaimed his victory over the devil and the demons.[5] Some suggest that Christ liberated the righteous souls who were in the "paradise" part of Hades and thus "led captivity in his train" (Eph. 4:8–10). That particular line of teaching has never seemed very likely to me. I think that the "captivity led captive" might refer to the public humiliation of the demonic forces mentioned in Colossians 2:15. Certainly, the Bible indicates that by his death and resurrection, Jesus won a great victory over the devil. It is possible that the harrowing of hell might be referred to in 1 Peter 3:18–21, a notoriously difficult passage to interpret. The only caveat I would issue is that this doctrine must not be used to suggest that Christ offered some kind of post-death salvation to people in hell. That simply is not a biblical idea. *"Behold, now is the day of salvation"* (2 Cor. 6:1–2 KJV). It is appointed to all of us to die once and after that to face the judgment (Heb. 9:27).

Setting aside speculation, the larger point remains. *The death of Christ brought startling changes in the spirit world, most of which remain hidden to us.* I think the Bible gives us hints and glimmers of the truth, just enough to let us know that something monumental happened "behind the scenes" as a result of Christ's death.

Heaven's Victory Parade

When Christ died, the demons were disarmed. Colossians 2:15 declares that "having disarmed the powers and authorities, he made a public spectacle of them, triumphing over them by the cross." To "disarm" someone means to take his weapons away. If a man has a gun pointed at you, he's not disarmed until you take the gun away from him. As long as he has the gun (and sufficient ammunition), you're in big trouble. When Jesus died on the cross, he took the guns and the ammo out of the hands of the demons. And he publicly humiliated them. Picture the Roman legions returning from a successful war. As they enter the city, vast throngs of women and children line the streets. On and on they march, a seemingly endless parade. Then come the victorious generals, each one accompanied by singers, dancers, and musicians. Finally at the end of the procession you spot a long line of weary, dirty, emaciated men. Their hands are tied, they shuffle one after another. They are the defeated soldiers, now brought back to be displayed as proof of Rome's invincible power.

When Jesus died, something stupendous happened in the spiritual realm. Although it was invisible to the naked eye, it was seen by all the angels and the Old Testament saints. They watched as Jesus, like some conquering Old West hero, entered the infernal regions and disarmed the "bad guys" one by one. Then he marched them in full view of his heavenly Father so that every created being would know that he had won the victory.[6]

This means that although demons have great power, they have been disarmed and cannot harm us unless we "rearm" them by our sinful compromise. Though they attack us, if we will use the "shield of faith" provided for us, every fiery dart will be quenched. Some Christians live in unnecessary fear of the demonic realm because they have never understood the victory Christ won for them. On the other hand, some believers suffer oppression because they nurse wrong attitudes and dabble with evil. That's like giving the devil a loaded gun and saying, "Why don't you go ahead and shoot me?" He'll always be glad to oblige you.

"Lo! His Doom Is Sure"

Finally, we learn that as a result of the cross Satan's doom is now guaranteed. In John 12:31, Jesus declares that "now the prince of this world will be driven out." In John 16:11, he adds that the "prince of this world now stands condemned." We learn of Satan's final end in Revelation 20:10, "And the devil, who deceived them, was thrown into the lake of burning sulfur." There he will be tormented "day and night for ever and ever" (v. 10).

That brings us to the end of the story. *At the cross Satan was disarmed, disgraced, and defeated.* The words of Martin Luther tell us what this means:

> And though this world with devils filled,
>   should threaten to undo us,
> We will not fear, for God hath willed
>   his truth to triumph through us.
> The Prince of Darkness grim,
>   we tremble not for him;
> His rage we can endure,
>   for lo, his doom is sure;
> One little word shall fell him.

What is that "one little word" that brings the devil down? It is the name *Jesus.* He fought the fight, he stood his ground, on the cross he utterly defeated Satan, and proved it by rising from the dead.

Having said all of this, one important question remains to be answered: *If Christ defeated Satan, why is there so much evil in the world?* In the words of a popular Christian book, Satan is alive and well on planet earth. He doesn't look very defeated to me. Certainly the devil seems to be having a field day. How else can you explain a woman suffocating her own children? How else can you explain three white men dragging a black man to death in Texas? How else do you explain evil in the high places, Satanism on the rise, and pornography like a filthy river flowing over the Internet?

He's Out on Bail

If Satan is defeated, he either doesn't know it or else he's taking the news very well. I put the matter that way because the New

Testament presents the truth about the devil in two different ways. On one hand, we are told over and over again that at the cross Satan was defeated as completely as anyone can be defeated. On the other hand, we are warned about the devil who roams about as a roaring lion, seeking someone to devour (1 Pet. 5:8). And we are told to put on the armor of God so we can stand in the evil day (Eph. 6:10–17). Is this not a contradiction?

I think the answer is no, but we need to do some careful thinking at this point. What happened at the cross was indeed the total defeat of Satan. In legal terms he was tried, found guilty, and sentenced to ultimate, eternal destruction. However, that sentence has not yet been executed, although there is no way for Satan to escape it. (Lo! his doom is sure.) Perhaps we should say that Satan is currently out on bail, wreaking havoc left and right, waiting for the day when he will be cast into the Lake of Fire once and for all. Until then he is destroying lives, breaking up homes, and disrupting God's work as much as he can.[7]

If you would prefer a military analogy, the cross was like D–Day in World War II. Once the Allies came ashore in Normandy, the German defeat was certain. Although much fighting would ensue and many soldiers would die, the Allies won the war on December 6, 1944. Satan's D-Day happened when Christ died on the cross. Since then his defeat has been certain, his ultimate surrender guaranteed. Meanwhile, he fights on in his desperate battle, a defeated but still dangerous foe.

Dealing with the Devil

If Satan is defeated but still dangerous, how should we deal with him? Here are a few quick suggestions:

1. *Stand and fight.* Ephesians 6:11–17 tells us to "put on the full armor of God," and it lists each piece of our personal

equipment. We are to put on this armor by faith so that when the day of battle comes, when temptation stares us in the face, when we feel like quitting, instead we can stand our ground, "and having done all, to stand" (KJV), meaning to stand victorious at the end of the day.

2. *"Resist the devil, and he will flee from you" (James 4:7).* This is both a command and a promise. If we will submit to God (the first part of the verse), we may be sure that when we resist the devil, he will flee from us. We have no power in ourselves against the devil, but he has no power to use against us when we fight with God's power. By ourselves we can't win; with God's help, we can't lose.

3. *Use the weapon of prayer.* My mind goes to that moment in the Garden of Gethsemane when Jesus wrestled with his fate. Knowing that he would soon bear the weight of the sin of the world, he prayed in agony, sweating as it were great drops of blood. So great was his abhorrence of sin that he asked God to take the cup from him. But even as he said the words, he knew that his Father could not grant that request. Then came the great relinquishment—"Not my will, but yours be done." Jesus won the victory in the Garden precisely because he poured out his soul to God. Let us not think that our battles will be won any other way. If the Son of God must agonize in prayer, how much more must we cry out to God.

4. *Renounce the devil and confess Christ openly.* Perhaps this is part of what Christ meant when he promised that whoever confesses him openly, he will acknowledge before the Father in heaven, and whoever denies him he will deny before the Father (Matt. 10:32–33). In the early days of the Christian church, baptismal candidates were asked, "Do you renounce the devil and all his works?" That same question is still asked today in many

churches before a believer is baptized. It is entirely biblical and should be asked of ourselves on a daily basis. While I do not believe in praying to the devil or "rebuking the devil" verbally (that is better left to the Lord Jesus Christ, in my opinion), I do believe it is entirely proper that when we pray we should renounce the devil and pray for God's help. Is this not what we mean when we pray, *"Lead us not into temptation, but deliver us from the evil one"* (Matt. 6:13)?

There is great hope at the end of the day for all those who struggle against sin. On Easter Sunday morning the word came down from heaven to the devil and all his demons: Turn out the lights, the party's over. Do you feel defeated? Stand and fight. Do you feel discouraged? Stand and fight. Have you been tempted to give in? Stand and fight. Are you wavering between right and wrong? Stand and fight. Remember this. The Captain of our salvation has already won the battle. Satan can harass you but he cannot destroy you. Lo! His doom is sure; one little word shall fell him.

A Truth to Remember: *On Friday it appeared that Satan had won the battle. On Sunday morning the true Victor walked out of the tomb, alive from the dead.*

Going Deeper

1. In what sense is Genesis 3:15 "the sum and summary of the whole Bible"?

2. "Satan can do nothing without God's permission." Do you agree? What comfort do you draw from this truth?

3. What difference does knowing Christ make at the moment of death?

4. According to Revelation 20:10, what is Satan's final destination?

5. What is your answer to the question discussed in this chapter: "If Christ defeated Satan, why is there so much evil in the world?"

6. Review the four steps to victory over the devil. Think of a practical way you can put each step into action this week.

*"For the message of the cross is foolishness to those who are
perishing, but to us who are being saved
it is the power of God."*
1 CORINTHIANS 1:18

chapter 11

The fool on the Hill:
what the cross Means to the world

I N HIS BOOK *THE CROSS OF CHRIST,*
John Stott points out that every religion and every ideology has
its own symbol. For the Buddhist it is the lotus flower. Judaism
has the Star of David and Islam the crescent. In this century the
communists were known for the hammer and the sickle and the
Nazis for the swastika. In our day the Democrats have the don-
key and the Republicans the elephant.

But in the beginning there was no recognized symbol for
Christianity. In the earliest days Christians recognized one
another by declaring "Jesus is Lord." It took several generations
for the cross to become the universal symbol of our faith. If you

visit the catacombs of Rome, you will discover the crude draw-
ings on the wall made by the earliest Christians in that city as
they retreated underground during times of persecution. They
drew pictures of Bible stories and they drew the fish, which
stood as a secret anagram for the Greek word IXTHUS—Jesus
Christ, Son of God, Savior. But in the earliest days they didn't
draw the cross. That would come later. The cross did not become
the common symbol of Christianity until the second century,
when the custom of making the sign of the cross on the forehead
arose. By the time of Emperor Constantine, the cross had
become well-established as "the sign" of the Christian faith.[1]

What makes it so odd is that the cross was one of the most
brutal means of execution ever devised. Unlike modern methods of capital punishment, which are designed to produce a
quick death, crucifixion was meant to guarantee that the person
on the cross would die a slow, agonizing death, sometimes
hanging on the cross until his bloated body fell to the ground.
And therein lies a paradox. *Christians worship a God who died on
a cross.* How can this be? When a familiar gospel song speaks of
the "old rugged cross, so despised by the world," it is sober
truth and not mere sentiment. If we dare to venture beyond the
stained glass, we discover that not everyone views the cross of
Christ with favor. The German philosopher Nietzsche called
Christianity a religion for weaklings. He mocked the idea of a
God who could be crucified.

During a debate between a Muslim and a Christian, the
Muslim apologist tried to ridicule the Christian faith by saying
that Christians are riding on the back of a crucified man. The
Christian gave the proper response: "You're right. We're riding on
the back of a crucified man, and he is going to take us all the way
to heaven." That illustrates a crucial difference in perspective. To

the world, the cross is a symbol of shame; to those who believe, it is a symbol of salvation.

What does the cross mean to the world? Here are three answers to that question.

Answer #1: The World Is Offended by the Cross

"But we preach Christ crucified: a stumbling block to Jews and foolishness to Gentiles" (1 Cor. 1:23). The Jews "stumbled" at the cross because most of them were looking for a political leader who would deliver them from the heel of the Roman Empire. Jesus dealt with this misunderstanding many times in his ministry, which is why he repeatedly told people not to spread the news of his miracles. He didn't want to start a political movement that would overthrow Rome. He intended to start a spiritual revolution that would overthrow Satan's power. At one point a group of people came to him and attempted to make him king by acclamation. He sent them away because he had no time or use for such things. He knew that seeking political power would be a distraction to his mission.

The Jews simply could not imagine a crucified Messiah. It is difficult for us to understand what crucifixion meant to the Jews. We've sanitized the cross and domesticated it. We gold-plate it and wear it around our necks. We put it on earrings and on our stationery. We hang ornate crosses in our sanctuaries and on our steeples. We build churches in the shape of the cross. All of this would have been unthinkable in the first century. So terrible was crucifixion that the word was not even spoken in polite company. If we want a modern counterpart, we should hang a picture of a gas chamber at Auschwitz in front of our sanctuary. Or put a noose there. Or an electric chair with a man dying in agony—his face covered, smoke coming from his head. The very thought sickens us. But that's what the cross meant for Jesus.[2] And that is why the Jews were scandalized by the cross. They could not conceive of a God who would allow his Son to die that way.

The Greeks were another matter. They didn't practice crucifixion so they didn't have the problems that the Jews did. They tended to look to philosophy as the answer to the deepest problems of life. The notion of a man hanging on a cross to save the world was utter nonsense to them.

Erwin Lutzer points out that the cross offends modern men and women in three ways. First, it offends our pride. The cross was and is a sign of weakness in the eyes of many people because it was a method for executing criminals. Only the worst of the worst, the dregs of society, so to speak, or the worst enemies of the state, were crucified. And we are called to follow a man who died on a cross! The thought is revolting. Yet that is exactly what God asks us to do, which in the minds of some people is like being asked to follow a loser. Second, it offends our wisdom. The cross spells the end to salvation by education, as if we could gain merit with God by sharpening our intellect so that we can answer the cosmic questions. This offends certain people who prefer to believe that the problem today is not sin, but ignorance. But they are wrong. Education is good and necessary, but it can never open the door of heaven. God purposely made the way of salvation simple so that young children could believe it, which is why Jesus said, "I tell you the truth, anyone who will not receive the kingdom of God like a little child will never enter it" (Mark 10:15). Third, the cross offends our values. It extends an equal invitation to the powerful and to the weak; it welcomes the flight attendant and the aborigine; it transforms the drug addict and the debutante. Anyone and everyone is invited into

God's family on exactly the same basis. There are no favorites and no special deals for those with money or power or worldly position. Those things that matter so much to us simply don't matter to God. This is a shocking affront to the way the world does business, but it is also the way of the cross.[3]

The world has not changed its opinions in two thousand years. The cross is still repugnant and offensive. In the last few years news reports have told of employees being threatened with dismissal if they wear a cross to work. Such a symbol is "offensive" to others who see it as some sort of threat that creates a hostile work environment. In the town where I live a Catholic hospital was prohibited from placing a lighted cross on top of its smokestack. Although the request for a zoning variance had been approved 4–0, the board of trustees voted it down, primarily because a lighted cross was "insensitive" to non-Christians. Never mind that this was a private symbol being erected on private property owned by a religious organization. One trustee, an atheist, objected because the cross reminded her of the prejudice she had experienced as a child. Many other examples could be given. After two thousand years the cross still sparks controversy and opposition because it points to a truth that many people do not want to hear.

Answer #2: The World Is Judged by the Cross

"For the message of the cross is foolishness to those who are perishing" (1 Cor. 1:18). The cross strikes at the heart of human pride. It announces in blood-red letters that you cannot save yourself— only God can save you.

No doctrine is harder to accept than the doctrine of human inability. This doctrine teaches us that there is nothing we can contribute to our salvation. We are so lost in our sins that we have no idea how sinful we really are. When we look into our own souls and see ourselves, we see only the sin that lies on the surface, but God sees to the bottom—and what he sees is a foul pit of iniquity. We are so lost that unless God takes the initiative to save us we will never be saved at all.

Isaiah 64:6 says that in the eyes of God "our righteous acts are like filthy rags" to him. Imagine taking your best dress or your best suit and dragging it through the mud. Then you put it on the floor where people can walk on it. Then you use it to mop up your dog's vomit. Then you put on the suit and drive to the most expensive restaurant in your town. What will they say when you come to the door? You will be immediately turned away. "But I have a reservation," you cry out. It matters not. You are not dressed appropriately to enter this fine restaurant. "Get out," the doorman says, "or I'll call the police." How do you think God feels when you stand before him dressed in the dirty rags of your own good deeds? What looks good to you is like a vomit-streaked dress in his eyes.

The cross stands as a silent sentinel proclaiming that you have to come God's way—or you won't come at all. Many people cling to the filthy rags of their own righteousness and then wonder why God won't take them in. The cross stands in judgment over the sinful pride of the human race. Just as Christ was stripped of his robe before he died, even so must we be stripped of ours.

When Christ died, he didn't die alone. Two thieves died with him. We often focus on the thief who cried out, "Remember me when you come into your kingdom." We know that man was saved because Jesus told him, "Today you will be with me in paradise" (Luke 23:43). But there was another man hanging beside Jesus. He cursed and swore and blasphemed the Son of God. He died as he had lived, a wretched sinner, unforgiven. Why did one believe and the other continue in his sin? There is no hint in the text that one man was "better" than the other. Both were hardened criminals. Both had the same opportunity to observe Christ as he was dying. They both heard his words of love and forgiveness. Both could have believed. Both could have rejected. But these two men, so alike on the outside, were different on the inside.

One thief was saved—that none would despair.

One thief was lost—that none would presume.

The cross that saved the one doomed the other. Jesus spoke of this truth when he declared, "Do not suppose that I have come to bring peace to the earth. I did not come to bring peace, but a sword" (Matt. 10:34). These words shatter the popular notion that Jesus came to make us feel better about ourselves. The exact opposite of that statement would be closer to reality. Jesus is the great divider of humanity. He came to turn "a man against his father" and "a daughter against her mother" (Matt. 10:35). As hard as those words sound, they come from the lips of Jesus himself, and we dare not ignore them or water them down. The cross judges the world—and every one of us individually—by confronting us with our sin, calling us to repentance, and challenging us to a higher allegiance than anything we have known before. And then to top it off, Jesus calls us to "take up the cross" and follow him. Those who will not do it are not worthy of him (Matt. 10:38). These are strong and even troubling words and most of us will spend a lifetime trying to understand what they mean, but those who choose the way of the cross, though it be filled with pain and difficulty, will save their lives. Those who reject the way of the cross will in the end lose all that they have lived for.

Jesus calls us *from* the cross, and he calls us *to* the cross. Those who will not heed his call will hate him all the more. And they stand condemned by the very cross that would have saved them.

Answer #3: The World Is Saved by the Cross

The last part of 1 Corinthians 1:18 declares that *"to us who are being saved it is the power of God."* What men call foolishness, God ordains as the instrument of salvation. What men mock, God raises up as the only means of salvation.

Nearly all of us know John 3:16. Let's go back two verses and see what leads into that most famous of all the biblical promises. *"As Moses lifted up the serpent in the wilderness, even so must the Son of man be lifted up"* (John 3:14 KJV). The first part of that verse refers to a strange moment in Israel's history recorded in Numbers 21. There we learn that during the wilderness wanderings, the people began to murmur against God and Moses. *"Why have you brought us up out of Egypt to die in the desert?"* (Num. 21:5). After forty years in the desert, they were tired of the heat and the sand and the long marches from one place to another. Even the manna seemed disgusting to them. Finally, they had had enough. God heard their complaint and sent fiery snakes among the people. Many were bitten and many died. Panic swept across the tribes. They came to Moses and said, "We were stupid to complain after all that God has done for us. Please pray to the Lord that he would remove these poisonous snakes." When Moses prayed to the Lord, he was instructed to make a bronze snake and put it on a tall pole where the Israelites could see it. Then God said, "Anyone who has been bitten, when he looks at it, shall live." And that's what happened. Anyone who looked, lived. Those who didn't, died.

What is the significance of the serpent? Recall that sin entered the human race through the serpent who deceived Eve (Gen. 3:1–6). Under ordinary circumstances, lifting up a serpent on a pole would be repulsive to the Jews. In this case it meant lifting up the symbol of the very thing that was killing them. John used this vivid image to teach us what the death of Christ really means. God took the hated symbol of Roman oppression and turned it into the means of our salvation. Here is the next verse—the verse before the most famous verse in the Bible, *"That everyone who believes in him may have eternal life"* (John 3:15).

When we read such a wonderful promise, we may wonder if "everyone" really means "everyone." While hosting a national call-in program, I spoke with a woman from Virginia who called with a good question. She wanted to know how we can know who the "chosen" of God are. My answer was very simple. We can't. Only God knows who the chosen (or the elect) are. Our calling is to preach the gospel to every man and woman on the face of the earth. We are to invite them to trust Christ and be saved. We aren't supposed to worry too much about who is elect and who isn't. God can take care of that himself. Our job is to preach the gospel and trust God to use the gospel to draw many people to faith in Christ. When I preach, I never know how people will respond or who will respond. I'm in sales, not administration. But that's true of all of us. We do the preaching and God does the drawing. When we do our part, God always does his.

I told the woman in Virginia that many years ago I heard someone say it like this. Imagine the gates of heaven with a sign over them reading, "Whosoever will may come." When you pass through those gates, you look back, and the sign reads, "Chosen from before the foundation of the world." I think there is good

biblical balance in that illustration. We are not called to "recon-
cile" predestination and free will. Only God can do that. Let us
preach the gospel with confidence, knowing that anyone who
trusts in the Christ who died on the cross and rose from the dead
will be saved.

God has no other plan of salvation—and he doesn't need
one. The same cross that offends the world and judges the world
also saves the world.

"Wow! That's Amazing!"

But there is a condition—*"whoever believes in him."* Even the
death of Christ cannot save you unless you believe in him. A
young girl named Angela asked how you can know you are
saved. I quoted 1 John 5:13, *"I write these things to you who believe
in the name of the Son of God so that you may know that you have
eternal life."* I told Angela that salvation depends on trusting
Jesus Christ. It's more than just believing facts about Jesus. Lots
of people do that. Even the demons believe in Jesus (James
2:19), but they are not saved. To trust in Christ means to rely
completely upon him. I told her that to trust in someone means
to put your life completely in the hands of that person. Trust is
what you do when you fly in a plane. You trust the pilot to get
you back down on the ground safely. You trust a doctor when
you take the medicine he prescribes. You trust a lawyer when you
let him represent you in court. God says that when you trust
Jesus Christ in that same way you are saved from your sins. It
means to trust Jesus so completely that if he can't take you to
heaven you aren't going to go there. All you have to do is trust
Christ completely and you can be saved. When I asked Angela
what she thought about that, she blurted out, "Wow! That's
amazing."

Yes it is. It's the most amazing truth I know.

More than once I have illustrated God's plan of salvation this way. Hold up your left hand and let it represent you standing before God with your sins unforgiven. Now hold up your right hand and cover it with a cloth or a towel or a handkerchief. Let your right hand represent Jesus Christ and the cloth, his perfect righteousness. As long as you (the left hand) stand before God with your sins uncovered, you cannot enter heaven. Now take both hands and clasp them together so that the cloth covers both hands. When God looks down from heaven, what does he see? He doesn't see your sins, because they are covered by the righteousness of Jesus Christ. Now you can enter heaven because God sees you as having the righteousness of his Son.

What does it mean to be "righteous" in God's sight? When God looks at me by myself, all he sees is my sin. And what I call righteousness, he calls filthy rags. I have nothing in myself that will pass for righteousness in his eyes. But when I place my trust in Jesus Christ—the great Lamb of God—then when God looks down from heaven, he sees "the Lamb over me" and declares me righteous in his eyes. How does this great blessing come to me? By faith alone. Not by anything I could ever do, but simply and only by faith in the crucified Lamb of God. All that I wanted but could never have, I find when I come to Jesus Christ. All that I wanted but could never achieve is provided for me by faith in the Son of God. What I lacked, he provided. What I wanted most, he supplied. What I needed, he freely gave.

In this chapter I have talked about what the cross means to the world. But I don't want to end on an abstract note. What does the cross mean to you? Is it just a religious symbol or a reminder of an ancient crucifixion? Is it something you wear around your neck? Or is the message of the cross stamped upon your heart?

The world is offended by the cross. If that is your situation, then I have nothing to say except that I pray God will change your heart. *The world is judged by the cross.* As long as you cling to the filthy rags of your own self-righteousness, the cross stands in judgment over you. *The world is saved by the cross.* This is our hope and this is our message to anyone who will listen.

In this life there are many roads a person may travel, but only one leads to heaven. The road to heaven starts at Calvary. Just keep walking in the blood-stained path of the crucified Savior and that road will take you safely home at last.

Going Deeper

Truth to Remember: *God has no other plan of salvation—and he doesn't need one. The same cross that offends the world and judges the world also saves the world.*

1. Name some ways in which the world is offended by the cross. Why do you think God picked such a hated symbol, the cross, as the way of our salvation?

2. Read Acts 17:16–34 (Paul's message on Mars Hill in Athens). What initial strategy did Paul follow when he came to Athens? How did he find common ground with the highly educated Athenians? How did they respond to his preaching?

3. How would you answer someone who says, "I believe there are many ways to God, and Jesus is just one of those ways"?

4. Read Numbers 21. What happened to those who looked at the brass serpent? To those who refused to look? How does this story point to the cross of Christ?

5. "I'm in sales, not administration." Why is this mind-set so important as we share Christ with others?

6. Think of several friends and loved ones who need to know Christ. What is keeping them from salvation? Spend some time praying for each person by name. Ask God to open each heart so they can respond to the gospel with true saving faith.

*"May I never boast except in the cross of our Lord Jesus Christ,
through which the world has been crucified to me,
and I to the world."*
GALATIANS 6:14

chapter 12

our crucified god:
what the cross means to the church

IT IS ONE OF THE IRONIES OF
history that the world rarely appreciates greatness the first time
around. It is only later, when time has given a clear perspective,
that we can sort out the heroes from the villains and the world-
changers from the big talkers. This is certainly true of Jesus
Christ. A *Newsweek* cover story summed up his immediate
impact this way:

> Historians did not record his birth. Nor, for 30
> years, did anyone pay him much heed. A Jew from
> the Galilean hill country with a reputation for
> teaching and healing, he showed up at the age of

33 in Jerusalem during Passover. In three days, he
was arrested, tried and convicted of treason, then
executed like the commonest of criminals. His followers said that God raised him from the dead.
Except among those who believed in him, the
event passed without notice.[1]

Everything in that paragraph is essentially correct. *When he
walked on planet earth, hardly anyone outside his own people knew he
was here.* After he left, it seemed that nothing had changed. And
yet we recently celebrated a new millennium, marking two thousand years since his birth. The entire world measures time by his
coming. He is the hinge on which history turns, the touchstone
of truth, the foundation of faith, and the final proof that God
exists.

The Passion Play

And yet it is true that inside the church the message has lost
its power to surprise us, perhaps because we have heard it so
many times before. Sometimes it helps to see it in a new light.
One year I preached just before Easter at Word of Life Florida, a
conference center located about an hour north of Tampa. One
afternoon I attended a performance of the passion play presented by students from the Word of Life Bible Institute. A passion play is a dramatic reenactment of the events surrounding
the death and resurrection of Christ. This particular production
featured lavish sets, high-tech sound and lighting, and some
amazing special effects. During the crucifixion scene, I watched
from the second row as the crowd on stage gathered to watch
Jesus being nailed to the cross. The music went on and on as the
angry throng shouted for Jesus to die. Tension rose as we all
wondered what had happened. Why was it taking so long to

crucify Jesus? The music swelled alongside the jeers of the mob. Surely something had gone wrong. Then without warning came the sound of spikes driving into the wooden crossbeam. Seconds later the crowd parted and the cross began to rise from the ground. There was Jesus hanging on the cross, just a few feet away from me, covered with blood, beaten nearly to death, his face disfigured, nails apparently driven through his hands, the crown of thorns shoved into his scalp, the scars from the scourging clearly visible. And the crowd! The laughing, mocking, crowd. Cheering as the Son of God dies a horrible death.

When I saw his face, I wanted to look away. I understood, perhaps for the first time, why the disciples fled from the scene. If I had been there, I would have run away too. Who could bear to look upon that sight? That is the shocking power of the cross of Christ. To see the cross, to really see it as if for the first time, is to be changed forever.

> See from his head, his hands, his feet
> Sorrow and love flow mingled down.
> Did e'er such love and sorrow meet?
> Or thorns compose so rich a crown?

In the last few chapters we have looked at the cross of Christ from different perspectives—what it meant to God, to Christ, to Satan, and what it means to the world. Now we look at the question in a more personal way: What does the cross mean to the church? Galatians 6:14 contains an important answer: "May I never boast except in the cross of our Lord Jesus Christ, through which the world has been crucified to me, and I to the world." The Apostles' Creed declares, "I believe in Jesus Christ who was crucified." When we say those words, we mean that the Son of God was murdered on a Roman cross at a place called Skull Hill outside the city walls of Jerusalem. We believe it literally happened—that if you and I had been there, we would have seen with our own eyes the slow, agonizing death of Jesus of Nazareth. We would have witnessed the humiliation of Christ as he died between two thieves, we would have seen the blood drip from his wounds, we would have heard him cry out, "My God, my God, why have you forsaken me?"

"He Took My Place—He Died for Me"

It was a horrible way to die, yet that is how the Savior of the world ended his life. But it is not the physical sufferings of Jesus that the Bible emphasizes. Rather, the biblical writers focus on what his death accomplished. We all know that he died for others. But what does that really mean? Perhaps an illustration will help. At the time of the Civil War there was a band of organized outlaws in the Southwest called Quantrill's Raiders. They would sweep down upon an unsuspecting community on the frontier, rob, pillage, burn, then ride away before help could come. The situation became so desperate that some people in Kansas formed a militia to search out the desperados. They had orders to execute without delay any of the raiders that could be found. Not long afterward a group of these men were captured. A long trench was dug; they were lined up, hands and legs tied, and eyes bandaged. The firing squad was forming. Suddenly a young man rushed out of the underbrush, crying out: "Wait! Wait!" Covered by the guns of the firing squad, he approached the officer in command. He pointed to a man who was waiting to be shot and said: "Let that man go free. He has a wife and four children and is needed at home. Let me take his place. I am guilty."

It was an extraordinary appeal, but the stranger insisted that it not be denied. After a long consultation, the officers decided to grant the request. They cut the ropes and released the condemned man. The volunteer was put in his place, and fell dead before the firing squad. Later the redeemed man came back to the awful scene of death, uncovered the grave, and found the body of his friend. He put it on the back of a mule and took it to a little cemetery near Kansas City, where he was given a proper burial. There he erected a memorial stone upon which were inscribed the words: *He Took My Place: He Died for Me.*[2]

This story is about one guilty man dying in the place of another. But something much greater happened at the cross. There a truly innocent man died, the just for the unjust, that he might bring us to God. When Jesus died, he took your place and suffered the penalty meant for you. He who was innocent paid the price that you might go free. This is truly beyond human understanding. As Romans 5:7 notes, perhaps for a righteous man some would dare to die. But who would die for sinners? Only God's Son would do a thing like that.

The Implications of the Cross

What are the implications of the cross for us today? In the Bible the cross is always a place of suffering and death. In a practical sense it means four things to the believer:

Death to the old life—Romans 6:6 and 1 Peter 2:24

Death to self—Galatians 2:20

Death to the flesh—Galatians 5:24

Death to the world—Galatians 6:14

The cross is essentially a confrontation with sin. The cross means that the old life is over and we can never go back to it again. It means there is a brand-new you. It means that we make a decisive break with sin and set out to follow Jesus day by day. The cross is God's way of saying, "You can have your sin or you can have my Son—but you can't have both." To die to the world means the things that used to seem so important—the drive for money, the compulsion to power, the need to dominate, the desire to win at any cost, the lust for sexual fulfillment, the desperate search for the approval of others—no longer rule your life. You live by a new standard and that means saying good-bye to the old way of life. Jesus said, "If anyone would come after me, he must deny himself and take up his cross daily and follow me" (Luke 9:23). Those words mean exactly what they say. Unless you deny yourself and enter by way of the cross, you are not a genuine disciple of Christ. "When you kneel at the cross, you will not hear an easy, soft word—not at first. Even though the cross is the only door to life, you are going to hear about death—death to every sin!"[3]

The Commands of the Cross

The New Testament gives us three commands of the cross. We dare not ignore these. If we do, we risk ceasing to be the church and simply becoming a religious social club. We are to . . .

1. Carry the cross—Luke 9:23
2. Boast in the cross—Galatians 6:14
3. Preach the cross—1 Corinthians 1:18–21

The first command is the key to everything else. The most basic commitment a disciple makes is to carry the cross. But what exactly does that mean? The words of Jesus make it clear: "If anyone would come after me, he must deny himself and take up his cross daily and follow me. For whoever wants to save his life will lose it, but whoever loses his life for me will save it. What good is it for a man to gain the whole world, and yet lose or forfeit his very self?" (Luke 9:23–25). The first disciples would have been shocked to hear that they had to carry a cross. That wasn't what they bargained for when they signed up to follow

Jesus. No self-respecting person would voluntarily carry "his cross." Only condemned criminals carried a cross, and it meant they were about to die. What could it possibly mean to carry your cross "daily"? What did that have to do with following Jesus? Merrill Tenney explains why Jesus posed this challenge to his disciples: "The impending event of the cross made it necessary for them to declare their values. Would they, in the stress of the days before them, choose the safety and comfort of living for themselves? Or would they accept his values and adhere to him at all costs?"[4]

We all have choices to make. Every day we get out of bed and choose how we will spend the day. The point Jesus is making is that to follow him will seem in the eyes of the world as if you are wasting your life. The people of the world will never understand what you are doing. It will seem to them that by following Jesus, you are throwing your life away. And of course, there is always another option. You can try to save your own life by following your own desires. Lots of people do that. They live as if their career were all that mattered. But the people who live only for this life in the end will find that they wasted it on things that don't really matter. They try to save it by living for themselves but in the end they lose it. They have wasted their lives on trivial pursuits.

Christ invites us to follow him. But he offers us—not an easy road—but a cross! And not a safe, comfortable, padded cross, but a rough-hewn cross like his. As Dietrich Bonhoeffer pointed out, "When Christ calls a man, he bids him come and die."[5] In a strange way that makes no sense to the world and often makes no sense to others, and indeed often makes no sense to us. The call of Christ is to come and die with him every single day. That means dying to our selfish desires, our own limited agendas, our own stunted dreams, our own foolish whims, our own short-sighted plans. If we follow Christ, he promises us—get this!—he promises—no! he guarantees us—that the road will be hard, the way difficult, the opposition fierce, and our companions uncertain. This is his invitation, and this is what he means when he calls us to take up our cross daily and follow him. If we follow him, he will lead us back to Skull Hill day after day after day. There we will die with him, and there our plans and hopes and dreams will die as well.

But that's only half the story. In the end, Jesus says, you will save your life. The people who laugh at you now won't be laughing then. They will see that you were right and they were wrong. What good will it do if you become the richest man in the world or climb to the top of the corporate ladder or rise to the highest salary level in your company or win the applause of the world, if in the end you find out it was all wasted? What good will that shiny new Mercedes do for you then? Will you be able to trade it in for another life? No, you won't. But if you want to live that way, go ahead. Millions of people do. In the end they will be sorry, but by then it will be too late to do anything about it.

Each one of us has a choice to make. Will we take the way of the cross or the way of the world? You've got to invest your life somewhere. What's the best deal you can make? Jesus made it clear why he did what he did when he said, *"Except a grain of wheat fall into the ground and dies, it remains alone. But if it dies, it brings forth much fruit"* (John 12:24, adapted from KJV). Out of one seed comes forth a vast harvest, but that seed must die in order to bring forth fruit. As long as the seed "saves" its life, it remains alone. But when it "loses" its life in death, it brings forth the harvest. It's simple, really. If you try to "save" your life, in the end you "lose" it. But if you dare to "lose" it for Jesus' sake, in the end you "save" it. Jesus himself is the supreme example of this principle.

Here's the bottom line: Taking up your cross means at a very profound level to reject the world and its values and to follow Jesus wherever he leads, whatever the cost.

Offered Up for Christ

Tucked away in Philippians 2 is a beautiful picture of how this principle works out in practice. Although Paul is writing from a jail in Rome where he is under a twenty-four-hour guard, his heart is filled with joy because he knows that his chains have served to advance the gospel. Through him the gospel is spreading throughout the palace guard and other Christians are gaining courage from his brave example (Phil. 1:12–14). But that's only part of the story. Paul explains his motivation this way: "That I may boast on the day of Christ that I did not run or labor for nothing. But even if I am being poured out like a drink offering on the sacrifice and service coming from your faith, I am glad and rejoice with all of you. So you too should be glad and rejoice with me" (Phil. 2:16b–18). Paul envisions a day when he will stand before the Lord Jesus Christ and give an account of his ministry. In that day his greatest desire is to be able to boast about what the Philippians had done for their own generation.

What will you boast about when you stand before the Lord? Your job . . . a big bank account . . . a new house . . . all the important people you know? Do you think that will impress the Lord Jesus Christ? I don't think so. In that day the only thing that will matter is the people you brought with you to heaven. Everything else will fade away.

Paul mentions being "poured out like a drink offering" on their behalf. This refers to the Old Testament practice of pouring wine on top of an animal sacrifice so that the heat of the fire immediately vaporizes the wine, turning it into a beautiful aroma. He is saying, "Even if I end up losing my life for you, it won't matter to me as long as you live for Christ." With that statement we come to the bottom line of Christian service. I wonder how many of us can truly say that it doesn't matter whether we live or die so long as the people we know follow the Lord?

The Missionary Graveyard

During a trip to Nigeria several years ago, my wife and I visited the Miango Rest Home a few miles outside the city of Jos. The term *rest home* conveys a particular image in America. In Nigeria it means something like a church camp or a conference center. It's a lovely spot in a rural area—a perfect place for missionaries to rest from their labors. As we walked across the grounds, we came to a lovely fieldstone church called Kirk Chapel. It is a quiet place, an oasis, a place to meet God. Behind the church there is a missionary graveyard containing about sixty graves of men and women who made the ultimate sacrifice for the sake of the gospel. Half or more of the graves are children— most of them dying in the first few days or weeks of life. I was told that in the early part of the twentieth century the life expectancy of a missionary to Africa was only eight years.

I saw a grave with a man's name and then the dates— 1919–1953. The marker read, "Placed in loving memory by his wife and children"—then giving their names. Underneath were two words—"Abundantly Satisfied." One of the newest graves contains a thirteen-year-old girl who had died two years before in a car wreck. When my wife visited the graveyard early on Sunday morning, she saw the mother standing silently at her daughter's grave. The inscription reads, "She is with her best friend and Lord, Jesus."

So many markers. Here is a child who died after one day. Then another one who lived a few days. And over here are a father and son buried side by side. He died trying to rescue his son from an overflowing creek. Both drowned.

Why would God allow this to happen? Why would he permit such suffering for his servants who sacrificed so much for the gospel? And why would he take the lives of little children? The parents had a choice in the matter; the children didn't. They didn't ask to come to Africa. But now they are buried there. I do not know the answers to any of these questions.

The missionary graveyard at Miango sends this message: *God's grace is free, but it is never cheap.* The missionaries and their children buried there bear testimony to the high cost of the Great Commission. Reaching the world has never been easy, and Jesus knew that it wouldn't be. That's why he said, "In this world you will have trouble" (John 16:33). It was true in the beginning, and it is still true today. I noted that the newest grave at Miango contained the body of a stillborn child—placed there just five months earlier, the daughter of one of the surgeons at the Evangel Hospital in Jos.

Many centuries ago Tertullian declared that "the blood of the martyrs is the seed of the church." How true. Wherever the church has gone, the cost of a new field has always been paid in blood. I saw a marker at Miango for a little child—a boy, I think—who died in the 1950s. The inscription read something like this: "We plant this seed in the hope that it will someday bear a harvest of souls for the kingdom."

When I walked back to my room, my eyes wet with tears, I said to my wife, "When I think of how little I have placed on the altar . . ." I could not finish the sentence. Compared to these men and women, I have made no sacrifice for Christ at all.

And what can we say about those who are buried in the missionary graveyard? My mind ran to Hebrews 11:35–38 and its list of tragedies for those who lived by faith. "Others were tortured and refused to be released . . . . Some faced jeers and flogging, while still others were chained and put in prison. They were stoned; they were sawed in two; they were put to death by the sword. They went about in sheepskins and goatskins, destitute, persecuted and mistreated" (vv. 35–37). And then this wonderful phrase: "The world was not worthy of them."

Does it seem like too much? Does it seem as if the price was too high to pay? Before you answer, remember what God did when he sent his Son to the world. Think of what it cost him to provide salvation for a human race that had turned against him. God also buried his Son on the mission field.[6]

The Power of the Cross

We must lift up the cross because it is the only message we have. If we talk about politics, we may get a new leader in the White House, but we won't change the hearts of people. All around us are people who carry a heavy weight of sin. They are sick in their hearts from the burden they carry. You can see it in their eyes, read it in their faces, hear it in their voices. They long for something better, they wonder how they can be free of their sin. Where can they go?

The story is told of an old Spartan who tried in vain to make a corpse stand upright. But after failing time and again, he declared, "It wants something within." How true for all of us. That is what we all want—we want something within. We want a power that can break the chains of sin. We want a power that can enable us to stand upright, to run and not be weary, to walk and not faint. Where can we find such a power within? Only in the cross of Christ.[7]

All that we believe is wrapped up in the cross of Christ. It is the central truth of the Christian faith and the preeminent event of human history. The cross is our message, our hope, our confidence. It is our badge of honor and the emblem of suffering and shame. Though the world despises the cross, we rally to it. In this sign, and this alone, we will conquer. Therefore, let us love the cross, preach the cross, stand by the cross, and never be ashamed of the cross. Hold it high as the banner of our salvation. Lift it up as the hope of the world. There is no power greater than the power of the cross. It is the only power that can lift men and women out of their sins, release them from condemnation, give them new life, and set their feet in a new direction.

Christianity is supremely the religion of the cross. Though the world may not want to hear it, we must preach it over and over—and then urge men and women to run to the cross of Christ. When we preach Christ crucified, rebel souls will lay down their weapons and join us in worshiping him as Savior and Lord.

Going Deeper

1. In your opinion what two or three factors best explain the amazing growth of Christianity in the last two thousand years?

2. How does coming to Christ separate you from the world and its evil desires? In what ways have you seen this principle at work in your own life?

3. How would you counsel a person who says he wants to follow Jesus but doesn't want to make any changes because he is happy with his life as it is?

A Truth to Remember: *Taking up your cross means at a very profound level to reject the world and its values and to follow Jesus wherever he leads, whatever the cost.*

4. "When Christ calls a man, he bids him come and die." Do you agree? If this is true, why would anyone want to follow Christ?

5. Consider the story of the missionary graveyard. What does it teach us about the cost of the Great Commission?

6. In personal terms, what does it mean to you to take up your cross daily and follow Christ?

"For we know that our old self was crucified with him so that the body of sin might be done away with, that we should no longer be slaves to sin."
ROMANS 6:6

chapter 13

free at last!
The cross and our sin

THERE ARE MANY REASONS people give for not becoming a Christian. Most of those reasons are in the form of either excuses or misunderstandings. But there is at least one reason that bears some consideration.

The woman said, "Pastor, you don't understand. I've been like this for so many years, I don't think I can ever change." The man said, "You've never been in the grip of alcohol. You don't know what it's like to go for years and never miss a day without a drink. I don't think it's possible for me to change." "I can't forgive her," he said, "not after what she did." The woman said, "I can't forgive him." They all say, "Don't give me that Jesus stuff. Nothing will ever change."

Question: Is real change possible?

You already know what the answer is supposed to be, so let's get down to reality. Is real change possible? Maybe it is, maybe it isn't. Lots of people think the answer is no. Lots of Christians fear the answer is no.

In this chapter I'm going to tell you that real change is possible, but you don't have to believe it. In fact, I don't blame you if you say, "I've heard all this before." Especially if you have never come to Jesus Christ by faith, you have every reason to doubt whether real change is possible. You don't have to take my word for it. The invitation of the gospel is always the same: "Come and see." Come and see for yourself. Make up your own mind. Decide for yourself whether Jesus Christ can make a difference.

Is real change possible? Can the leopard change its spots? Can a person whose life has been going in one direction suddenly go another direction? Can a person who has lived in the grip of debilitating sin for decades find liberation? The Christian faith says yes. *In fact, if that's not true, then there is no such thing as the Christian faith.* We're all just playing a religious game.

Two Key Words

In thinking about the possibilities of lasting change, it helps to focus on two crucial theological terms: *justification* and *sanctification*. The first word describes what happens when God declares us righteous in his eyes. If you have a computer, you know that by pushing a button you can have "justified" right margins, or margins that are straight from top to bottom. To be justified means to be declared straight in the eyes of a holy God. When God looks at you, he doesn't see the crookedness of your life; he sees that you have been credited with the perfection of Jesus Christ. This is a wonderful miracle that takes place the moment a person trusts Jesus Christ as Savior. In the act of coming to God through Christ, a great transaction takes place in the accounting room of heaven. Your sin is reckoned or counted or imputed to the Lord Jesus Christ, and his perfect righteousness is imputed or counted or reckoned to you. Justification then is an event that takes place in heaven, not on earth. It changes your standing before God. The guilt of your sin is removed and you are credited with the righteousness of Jesus Christ. It isn't something you feel or experience, yet it is absolutely true because it is based on the promise of God (see, for instance, Rom. 4:5).

However, one huge problem remains. While you are "reckoned" as a saint by God because you are credited with the righteousness of Jesus Christ, you are still a sinner. Justification changes your *standing,* not your *state.* Even after coming to Christ, you still maintain an inner desire to sin. The things that tempted you before will probably still tempt you after you are saved. This can be a disconcerting reality for many people who sincerely thought or hoped or prayed that by coming to Christ all their problems would be solved. The opposite is much more often true. Coming to Christ solves your greatest problem—your need for forgiveness, the certainty of eternal life, and your deep need for a relationship with God—but it doesn't permanently solve the reality of sin in your life.

That's where the second word comes in. Sanctification describes that process whereby God takes forgiven sinners and progressively makes them holy. Justification is that act whereby God declares you righteous in his eyes. Sanctification is that act whereby God makes you righteous. But those things are not the same:

Justification occurs when you trust Christ and is
never repeated.
Sanctification occurs continually as you surrender your life to the Lord.

Justification delivers from the *penalty* of sin.
Sanctification delivers from the *power* of sin.

Justification is an *event*.
Sanctification is a *process*.

Justification happens *once and only once*.
Sanctification is *gradual and continuous*.

Justification *cannot* be repeated.
Sanctification *must* be repeated.

Justification is the work of a *moment*.
Sanctification is the work of a *lifetime*.

Justification gives you the *merit* of Christ.
Sanctification gives you the *character* of Christ.

These two doctrines are distinct yet inseparably related.
Justification leads to sanctification. Those who are truly born
again are led of the Spirit into a life of growing holiness. And
both justification and sanctification are gifts from God that flow
to us from the cross of Jesus Christ. Romans 6:1–7 tells of the
changed life that must issue from a new relationship with God
based on the death of Christ.

A Curious Question

Paul begins with a question, "What shall we say, then? Shall
we go on sinning so that grace may increase?" (Rom. 6:1). That
seems like an odd question, doesn't it? In order to understand it
properly, we need to discuss antinomianism. That's a word that
is itself made up of two shorter words—*anti* meaning against,

and *nomos* meaning the law. An antinomian is a person who is "against the law." Antinomianism describes a point of view that we might call "spiritual lawlessness." An antinomian is a person who wants to live life unencumbered by any rules whatsoever. He follows the credo "only believe and do as you please." This is the person who says, "I know I'm going to heaven when I die, therefore it doesn't matter how I live in the meantime"; or, "As long as I am a Christian, I am free to do whatever I want." Not only does this person not want the Ten Commandments; he doesn't want any commandments at all. *He claims to love God while at the same time living in sin.* He claims to follow Jesus but doesn't want to live by his teachings.

Evidently some believers in the early church were teaching that once you were justified, you were free to live as you please. This perverted view of Christian liberty led some people to claim that by sinning they were actually increasing the grace of God, because when they sinned, God forgave them, and thus their sin increased God's grace! It's a clever, sneaky way of justifying wrongdoing.

An antinomian says, "If I sin, it is covered by the grace of God. Therefore, my sin doesn't really matter very much because I know God will forgive me no matter what I do." Where does such thinking lead? To such statements as these:

- "I might as well commit adultery because God will forgive me."
- "I can blow my top because God will forgive me anyway."
- "I can be a lazy glutton because God will forgive me anyway."
- "It doesn't matter whether I tell the truth. I can always ask forgiveness later."

- "I can get angry, bitter, hostile, and upset because I know God still loves me."

We all think like that some of the time. My point is that whenever those thoughts come to us, at that point we are not thinking like biblical Christians. We are abusing the grace of God. John Watson offers this warning: "If any man be certain of condemnation in this world and in the one to come, it is the man who proposes to make the sufferings of Christ the shelter of his own sins and the Son of God the servant of iniquity."[1]

That way of thinking is probably the one great objection to the doctrine of eternal security. "If you believe you can never lose your salvation, why not go out and live in sin? After all, you know you're going to heaven." Unfortunately, some believers have done exactly that. They have engaged in grossly sinful behavior and dismissed it because they believe their salvation is still secure. Nevertheless, that does not disprove the doctrine of eternal security, which I believe Romans 8 clearly teaches. It does teach us something about the deceitfulness of the human heart.

So the question is, Why not "live it up" in sin so God can forgive us later?

A Very Strong Answer

"*By no means!*" The Greek literally says, "May it never be." It's Paul's strongest negative interjection. The King James Version catches the flavor of this phrase with the translation, "God forbid." We can think of other words that fit, such as "Impossible!" "Absurd!" "Nonsense!" "God forbid that we should ever begin to think like that."

Here's the reason Paul reacts so strongly: "*We died to sin; how can we live in it any longer?*" Underline the word *died*. That's the key word for us to think about. Paul's entire doctrine of the

Christian life hangs on the truth that we died to sin. Note the tense: We *died* to sin. That's a *past* tense. It refers to something that has already happened, not to something that needs to happen. This is not a present tense—"We are dying to sin"—or a future tense—"We will die to sin"—or an imperative—"Die to sin!" Nor is it an exhortation—"You should die to sin." This is a simple past tense—"You *died* to sin." The simple truth is that if you are a believer, you have already died to sin. It's a past event, an accomplished fact. What is a Christian? Someone who has died to sin.

But what does that phrase mean—"died to sin"? Here is a simple definition. It means that you have been set free from the ruling power of sin in your life. Romans 6 shows us sin as a vicious slave-master. Before you came to Christ, you were a slave to sin. Verse 2 is telling us that when you came to Christ, you were set free from sin's power (you "died" to sin's ruling power over you) and were placed under the rule of Jesus Christ.

Picture an ancient slave market. If you are a slave, you must obey your master's every word. He speaks, you obey. You are "alive" to his voice because he is your master. But suppose you are sold at an auction to a new master. From the moment of the sale, your old master no longer has any legal right to command you. He can speak, but you no longer have to obey. He can command, but you don't have to respond. You have "died" to his authority and "come alive" to a new master. Can you still obey the old master? Yes, but you don't have to, because he has no power over you unless you choose to give him power. It doesn't make sense to obey your old master when you have a new master.

That's the whole argument of Romans 6 in a nutshell. You "died" to your old slave master (sin) and have "come alive" to a new master (Jesus Christ). So why serve sin voluntarily when you don't have to? Why not serve Jesus Christ?

From B.C. to A.D.

To put it another way, if you are a Christian, your life has two parts—B.C. and A.D. Before Christ and After Deliverance. The story of your life is your transfer from the Before Christ side to the After Deliverance side. That's why the phrase in verse 6— "our old self was crucified with him"—is so crucial. Your "old self" is the life you used to live. It's the person you once were. It's the "old you" with your old way of thinking and acting and relating. All of that is gone now. It was crucified with Christ. You've gone from B.C. to A.D. Why would you want to live back in B.C.? You don't belong in that life anymore.

Why does Paul go into this in such detail? Because our tendency is to try to live in two worlds at once. We like to straddle the fence between the old life and the new life. We like to put one foot in the kingdom of sin and one foot in the kingdom of God. We like to have Christ *and* our old way of life. Paul says you can't do it. It won't work. It's not natural. You become spiritually schizophrenic. No one can live forever straddling the fence. Eventually you have to go one way or the other. It's easy for us to live this way, because we can justify a bad attitude or an abusive spirit or an evil habit or a lustful way of life or hidden idolatry or pride or arrogance or envy or any of a thousand other sins. We say, "It doesn't matter because I've got a foot in the kingdom so God has to forgive me." That's an abuse of the grace of God.

Talk like that reveals that you don't understand what Jesus did on the cross. It also shows that you don't understand what salvation really means. And it may possibly reveal that you've never truly been saved at all. One mark of a truly born-again person is a growing sensitivity to personal sin and a growing desire to please God.

You Can Sin—But You Won't Be Happy

Here is the truth about the Christian's relationship to sin: *The true believer cannot sin and stay happy.* You can sin, but you won't be happy. Or if you are happy, you won't stay happy. Sin and the believer are now mutually opposite. What once satisfied you no longer satisfies. Lust won't be as much fun. Anger won't be as satisfying. Pride no longer meets your inner needs. Where once you enjoyed nursing a bitter spirit, now it feels uncomfortable. Sin no longer "fits" your life. Oh, you can "wear" sin for a while, but it's like wearing old clothes that are two sizes too small. You can do it, but you won't be comfortable, you won't look natural, you won't feel right, and frankly, you won't look right either. Sin no longer "fits." Coming to Christ is like getting a whole new wardrobe. What fits now? Love, joy, peace, holiness, righteousness, compassion, zeal, concern for others. Those spiritual clothes fit just right. They were tailor-made for you. And those sins you used to wear so comfortably? They just don't fit any more. You feel awkward and you look goofy when you try to put them back on.

But what if you go back to the closet and put those old sins back on anyway? What happens to a Christian who chooses to sin? Let me give you three answers to that question:

1. *Your life won't work right.* The old clothes just don't fit anymore. You'll sin, but you won't receive any personal satisfaction.

2. *God will stop you.* He may judge you. He may discipline you. He will certainly arrange the circumstances so that your sin turns out to your own disadvantage. If you persist, he may even

take your life prematurely (cf. 1 Cor. 11:29–30; Heb. 10:26–31; 1 John 5:16–17).

3. If you persist in sin forever, it demonstrates that you were never truly saved. The operative word is *forever.* A true child of God may stay in sin for a long time, even for many years. But if you choose to sin, and never feel the call of God to repentance, and never feel the tug of the Holy Spirit bringing you back to God, your long-term spiritual indifference indicates in all likelihood that you were never saved in the first place.[2]

Direction Makes a Difference

If we graphed your spiritual experience, it would move up and down, up and down, up and down—but always moving in a generally upward direction. At any given moment, the graph of your life may show you relatively up or relatively down spiritually. You may be down for a long time, but if you know Jesus, eventually you will start moving up again. I draw two conclusions from this:

    1. Direction makes a difference.

    2. True believers move toward heaven.

Although we may fall into grievous sin, that's not where we belong, and we will not stay there forever. If you are a Christian, you won't be comfortable living in sin. The direction of your life will be away from sin and toward Jesus Christ. As the saying goes, "I would rather be one foot away from hell heading toward heaven than one foot away from heaven heading toward hell." Direction makes a difference.

Some people are saved one foot from hell. God turns them around at the very brink of the pit. When they are saved, they still have the smell of brimstone in their clothing. That's why new Christians sometimes look and act pretty rough. They've been snatched from the flames. Some of those same people will still look rough after five or ten years. That's OK because they started so low. You don't judge people by where they are now but by where they've come from yesterday. The only thing that matters is to keep moving in the right direction.

The direction of the true believer is always ultimately toward heaven. Sometimes we fly like the eagle. Sometimes we run with the stallions. Sometimes we walk in victory. And sometimes we're just stumbling upwards. I love that phrase—stumbling upwards. That's how the grace of God works.

His Death—And Ours

> Or don't you know that all of us who were baptized into Christ Jesus were baptized into his death? We were therefore buried with him through baptism into death in order that, just as Christ was raised from the dead through the glory of the Father, we too may live a new life (Rom. 6:3-4).

These verses are the *how* behind the answer of verse 2. They explain the vital doctrine of the believer's union with Jesus Christ. The key word is *baptism.* Through baptism we were united with Jesus and through him delivered from sin's power. *But that immediately plunges us into controversy.* What is this "baptism"? Is this water baptism? Or is it Holy Spirit baptism? The answer is yes! It is both, in the sense that whenever baptism is mentioned in the New Testament, water baptism is always in the picture somewhere. That is, when baptism was mentioned in the first century, the original readers would naturally think of water baptism. That was the rite of initiation into the Christian church. You were saved, then you were baptized, then you joined the company of believers (Acts 2:40-41).

However, it is also true that water baptism in the New Testament symbolizes certain spiritual truths. The word *baptize* means to immerse or to dip. The symbol behind the word is "identification." To totally immerse in water was a symbol of complete personal identification with Jesus Christ. Paul is not saying that the physical act of immersing in water somehow puts a person "in Christ." That happens the moment a person trusts Christ. Yet water baptism symbolizes perfectly that act of personal faith.

A Sermon Without Words

When I baptize people, I always tell the congregation that baptism is like preaching a sermon without saying a word. When a person stands in the water, he represents Jesus dying on the cross. When he is lowered into the water, he pictures Jesus being buried in the tomb. When he is raised out of the water, he symbolizes Jesus rising from the dead. So each time a person is baptized, he or she is "preaching" a sermon without saying a word. That truth is in the background of Romans 6. Paul uses the word *baptism* for the spiritual truth it symbolizes—our complete union with Christ in his death, burial, and resurrection. The moment we come to Christ, the Holy Spirit unites us with Christ in his death, burial, and resurrection. Water baptism is a divine object lesson that pictures that truth.

How does this fit into the larger argument of the passage? We can say it this way:

> 1. Should we continue in sin so that God's grace may abound?
> 2. God forbid! The very thought is absurd!
> 3. You died to sin. How can you live in it any longer?
> (Implied question: When did we die to sin?)

4. You died to sin when you were united with
Christ in his death. Your old life was buried with
him in his burial. You were raised from the dead
and given a brand-new life.

Let's think of this in a more dramatic way: It's 3:00 P.M. on a
hot Friday afternoon in Jerusalem. Three men hang on three
crosses. From a distance you cannot make out their faces. As you
come closer, the one in the middle seems strangely familiar. He
looks like someone you know. The eyes, the mouth, the tilt of
the head—it all seems so familiar. Who is this person in the middle? It looks like Jesus, but it, yes, the face looks like . . . no, it
can't be. You know it's Jesus, but the face . . . the face is yours!

You died on the cross with him!
You were buried in the tomb with him!
You rose from the dead with him!

You were there! That's what Paul is saying. By faith you are
spiritually joined to Christ in such a way that although two
thousand years separate you from Calvary, what happened to
him really and truly happened to you. How that can be is a mystery for the ages. Yet it truly is what the Bible teaches. And
because he was raised to new life, you were raised to new life.
Verse 4 uses a word that means a "brand-new" life, not just a better life. Salvation is not a "spiritual rehab." It's a full demolition
with a new foundation and a brand-new building.

Why Real Change Is Possible

Verses 5–7 spell out what this stupendous truth means for us
in our daily living.

United with Christ

"If we have been united with him like this in his death, we will certainly also be united with him in his resurrection" (Rom. 6:5). The word *united* means "joined at birth." It has the idea of being inseparably joined with Jesus. One commentator used the phrase "fused into one"—almost as if we were speaking of conjoined babies who share the same vital organs. How close are you to Jesus? If you know him, his life is your life, his strength is your strength, his mind is your mind, his power is your power.

The Old Self Crucified

"For we know that our old self was crucified with him so that the body of sin might be done away with, that we should no longer be slaves to sin" (Rom. 6:6). If this verse seems confusing, just concentrate on the last phrase. God's purpose in "crucifying our old self" was that "we should no longer be the slaves of sin." *God's purpose is clear: He wants to free you from slavery to sin.* In order to do that, he had to crucify (put to death) your old self. The New English Bible says, "We know that *the man we once were* was crucified with Christ." That happened the moment you believed. Your old life died. You may not have known it, or felt it, or been even slightly aware of it. You may not have asked for that or even wanted it to happen. Perhaps you thought that somehow you could keep Christ plus your old life. But it doesn't work that way. You can have Christ *or* your old life. Not both.

The phrase "body of sin" refers to your literal body as a helpless tool of sin. Sin worked through your tongue to say ugly words. Sin worked through your hands to commit foul deeds. Sin worked through your eyes to behold impure acts. Sin worked through your ears to listen to slander and gossip. Sin worked through your private parts to commit immorality. Sin worked through your feet to carry you to places you shouldn't go. Sin worked through your lips to eat to the point of gluttony and drink to the point of drunkenness. Without Christ, your body was truly a "helpless tool of sin." But now the power of sin has been broken. The phrase "done away with" literally means "rendered powerless." Like an engine with no spark plugs, like a motor with no ignition, like an appliance with no plug, your body can no longer be a tool of sin unless you choose to let it happen.

Able Not to Sin

Can we still sin? Yes. Is sin necessary? No. Is it inevitable? No. What makes a Christian sin? You sin when you choose to yield to the sin that indwells your body.

Augustine explained it this way:

> Adam before the Fall was . . . able to sin.
> Adam after the Fall was . . . not able not to sin.
> Believers in Christ are . . . able not to sin.
> In heaven we will be . . . not able to sin.[3]

Number three is where we live today. We are "able not to sin." But the choice is ours. Sin was defeated by Christ on the cross and exists today as a defeated foe. Sin indwells your body and still tries to control you. But we no longer need to yield to it, which means that sin cannot defeat us unless we choose to yield to it. In essence, we cannot be defeated unless we choose to be defeated. And Paul's whole point is—why would anyone *choose* to be defeated? To say it another way, victory is now possible. It is not inevitable. We still have responsible choices we must make. But before we came to Christ, we had no choice at all. We were slaves to sin whether we realized it or not.

Freed from Sin

"Anyone who has died has been freed from sin" (Rom. 6:7). This is the final and ultimate blessing of our union with Christ. We have been set free from sin. That means just what it says. We were enslaved to sin, but now through Christ we have been set free. Why, then, would we ever go back to sin? Only one answer seems possible. We go back to sin because we think it will make us happy. And we're right. Sin is fun for a while. Drunkenness is fun for a while, adultery is fun for a while, lust is fun for a while, anger satisfies for a short time, bitterness has its rewards, thievery is fun while you get away with it, gluttony is fun until you wake up the next morning feeling guilty. Sin gives pleasure but only for a short season. All Satan's apples have worms.

While preaching on this text, I made a passing comment like this: "You can be an alcoholic drunk and it's fun for a while." After the service a friend passed a note to me. "Pastor Ray, in your sermon you said alcoholic drunkenness is fun for a while. Wrong! Drunkenness is fun for a while until it becomes alcoholic drunkenness. And then it is a life of despair." My friend knows whereof she speaks. She knows the truth of her words, because she once lived in that despair. But Jesus Christ has delivered her and set her free from alcoholic drunkenness. By the power of Jesus Christ, she has been delivered from slavery to sin. Where once she knew only self-loathing and despair, now she knows freedom and full deliverance. She has died to sin and through Jesus Christ has been raised to a brand new life. She's living a different life now because she's not the person she used to be.

Jesus said, *"If the Son sets you free, you will be free indeed"* (John 8:36). Multitudes of believers can testify that they have been delivered from sin and set free indeed through Jesus Christ.

"He Breaks the Power of Canceled Sin"

One of Charles Wesley's most famous hymns says it well:

> O for a thousand tongues to sing
> > my great Redeemer's praise,
> The glories of my God and King,
> > the triumphs of his grace.
> Jesus! the name that charms our fears,
> > that bids our sorrows cease,
> 'Tis music in the sinner's ears,
> > 'tis life and health and peace.
> *He breaks the power of canceled sin,*
> > *he sets the prisoner free;*
> His blood can make the foulest clean;
> > his blood availed for me.
> My gracious Master and my God,
> > assist me to proclaim,
> To spread through all the earth
> > abroad the honors of thy name.

The first line of the third verse might stand as a summary of all we have said in this chapter: "He breaks the power of canceled sin, he sets the prisoner free." There are none so happy as those who have been set free by Jesus Christ. Rejoice, child of God, the charges have been dropped, the chains now broken, the cell door opened. You are free. Why would you ever go back to prison?

Will You Go Back? God Forbid!

Will a prisoner go back to prison? God forbid!
Will a slave go back to his master? God forbid!
Will a rich man return to his poverty? God forbid!
Will a happy man go back to sadness? God forbid!

Will a survivor go back to a concentration camp?
    God forbid!
Will a Christian go back into sin? God forbid!

Paul says, "God forbid!"
The Bible says, "God forbid!"
The church says, "God forbid!"
The angels say, "God forbid!"
The Holy Spirit says, "God forbid!"
Let all God's people say, "God forbid!"

One of the Puritan preachers was speaking on this text several hundred years ago. He said the accusation is often made against the church that we preach a gospel that leads to loose living. So he asked his people, "Is there anybody here who has been living such a life that you have given other people an excuse not to believe in Jesus?" Great question. He then observed that one man who lives a loose life does more harm than the good ten holy men do by their righteousness.[4]

One Sunday a woman came to me in tears saying, "Pastor, I have not been living the kind of life that would be pleasing to God." We prayed together and asked God to make her effective for Jesus so that she might be a light in the darkness. It is precisely at this point that the cross of Christ becomes a powerful motivation for godly living. If we live in sin, we have only ourselves to blame. If we go back to the old life, it will not be because Jesus Christ failed somehow. In the cross we find everything we need to live a new life. We find the power to say no to sin and yes to God, and we also find in the cross the example of one who loved us enough to die for us. A verse from a famous hymn by Isaac Watts says it well:

Were the whole realm of nature mine,
That were a present far too small;
Love so amazing, so divine,
Demands my soul, my life, my all.

I began by asking this question: Is real change possible? Through Jesus Christ the answer is yes. You've been set free. If the course of your life has been downward, it doesn't have to stay that way. By the grace of God, your life can be different. The happiest people you will ever meet are those who have turned their backs on sin and set their feet on the road to heaven.

Going Deeper

A Truth to Remember: *If we go back to the old life, it will not be because Jesus Christ failed somehow. In the cross we find everything we need to live a new life.*

1. According to this chapter, what is the difference between justification and sanctification? Is it possible to ever reach a point in this life where you are completely sanctified?

2. What is antinomianism? Give several examples of ways that professing Christians abuse the grace of God.

3. In what sense did we die with Christ two thousand years ago? Why is that such an important truth for the Christian life?

4. If we truly are "able not to sin," why do we sin at all?

5. In what areas of your life are you making wrong choices that lead you back into spiritual bondage?

6. "The direction of the true believer is always ultimately toward heaven." Do you agree? What is the current direction of your life?

"Then I saw a Lamb, looking as if it had been slain,
standing in the center of the throne."
REVELATION 5:6

chapter 14

worthy is the lamb:
The cross in heaven

SOME DAY YOU WILL READ IN THE papers that D. L. Moody, of East Northfield, is dead. Don't you believe a word of it! At that moment I shall be more alive than I am now. I shall have gone up higher, that is all; out of this old clay tenement into a house that is immortal—a body that death cannot touch; that sin cannot taint; a body fashioned like unto his glorious body. I was born of the flesh in 1837. I was born of the Spirit in 1856. That which is born of the flesh may die. That which is born of the Spirit will live forever." During his evangelistic campaigns D. L. Moody loved to quote the first two sentences as a way of shocking his audiences with the truth that death would not be the end of his life but only the beginning.

His words came true on Friday, December 22, 1899. After decades of nonstop preaching, writing, speaking, evangelizing, and traveling, his heart finally began to fail. With his family gathered around, he cried out, "Earth recedes; heaven opens before me." His family thought that perhaps he was dreaming. Then he spoke to one of his sons: "No, this is no dream, Will. It is beautiful. It is like a trance. If this is death, it is sweet. There is no valley here. God is calling me, and I must go." Then it seemed as if he saw heaven opened before his eyes. "This is my triumph, this is my coronation day! I have been looking forward to it for years." His face lit up. "Dwight, Irene—I see the children's faces." He was speaking of the two grandchildren who had died the previous year. A few minutes later he took his last breath. Thus did D. L. Moody enter heaven. He died as he had lived, full of faith and ready to meet the Lord.[1]

I'd Rather Go to North Carolina

Children have no trouble believing in heaven even though their ideas are sometimes a bit mixed up. Many of them think heaven is some sort of celestial amusement park where you can ride on the ferris wheel and eat ice cream all day long and never get sick. Other children picture heaven as a kind of unending church service that goes on and on and on and never seems to stop. One seven-year-old boy spoke for many adults when he said, "I know what heaven is, but I don't want to go there. I want to go to North Carolina instead."

Many of us would say the same thing. We know heaven is real, but we'd rather go to North Carolina (or Florida or Hawaii) first. Heaven can wait as far as we're concerned. But that attitude, common though it may be, reflects a complete reversal of the biblical picture. This earth is passing away. It is here today and gone tomorrow. Heaven (which seems almost like a fairy tale to us) is the true reality, and it is "the heart's true home."

The Book of Revelation tells us more about heaven than any other book in the Bible. Most of us probably know about the lovely picture of heaven in Revelation 21 and 22, but there is another picture of heaven found in Revelation 5. In only fourteen verses the apostle John pulls back the curtain and gives us a tantalizing glimpse of our eternal home. Here we discover that the cross of Christ will still be our focus in eternity. This rare glimpse of heaven displays the victory of the Lamb who was slain.

"Who Is Worthy to Open the Book?"

> Then I saw in the right hand of him who sat on the throne a scroll with writing on both sides and sealed with seven seals. And I saw a mighty angel proclaiming in a loud voice, "Who is worthy to break the seals and open the scroll?" But no one in heaven or on earth or under the earth could open the scroll or even look inside it. I wept and wept because no one was found who was worthy to open the scroll or look inside (Rev. 5:1–4).

The place: the throne room of heaven. The time: sometime in eternity. The setting: a magnificent throne and a mysterious scroll. Around the throne are myriads of angelic creatures, glorious and awesome to behold. A bright rainbow encircles the throne. Surrounding the throne are twenty-four elders wearing crowns of gold. Peals of thunder roll from the throne, flashes of lightning frame the one seated there. The throne is surrounded by a sea of glass, clear as crystal. Everywhere there is singing, worship, and praise. Your eye darts from one detail to another.

You notice the four living creatures and wonder who they are and what they represent. There are armies of angels on every hand. There are cherubim and seraphim and other angels you cannot identify. There is smoke and incense and light and joy. Your eyes and ears cannot take it all in. "Holy, Holy, Holy" cry the four living creatures. Suddenly, spontaneously, gladly, you find yourself bowing down before the one on the throne.

You have come to heaven at last. You are in God's presence. *So this is what it is like,* you think to yourself. It was nothing like you expected but everything you dreamed, and much, much more. Nothing you heard or saw or imagined on earth prepared you for this moment, yet you feel strangely at home. Or perhaps not so strangely, for now at last you are home. Home where you belong. At home with the Lord.

After a few moments (or an hour? or a day? or a month? or a year? time doesn't seem to be the same in heaven) your eyes return to the scroll in the hand of him who sits on the throne. What is the scroll? It appears to be a long parchment, with writing on both sides, sealed with some sort of wax. It could be some sort of legal document, like a title deed. In that case, only the owner could open it. While you ponder the scroll and wonder what it means, an angel cries out, "Who is worthy to break the seals and open the scroll?" There is silence in heaven. No one steps forward. No one in all the universe is worthy to open the scroll or look inside it. What a strange sight this is. A scroll that no one can open.

Then one of the elders speaks up: *"See, the Lion of the tribe of Judah, the Root of David, has triumphed. He is able to open the scroll and its seven seals"* (Rev. 5:5). Judah was the tribe from which the Messiah would come (Gen. 49:8–10). The "Lion" of the tribe of Judah speaks of its greatest son who combined within his own being power, wisdom, majesty, greatness, and ultimate regal authority. He is also called the "Root of David," a term meaning that he is a direct descendant of David, Israel's greatest king. But who is this "Lion" who is also called the "Root of David?" Verse 6 states: "Then I saw a Lamb, looking as if it had been slain, standing in the center of the throne, encircled by the four living creatures and the elders. He had seven horns and seven eyes, which are the seven spirits of God sent out into all the earth." As you look toward the great throne, there in the center of the angelic creatures and the twenty-four elders is a Lamb. But not an ordinary lamb. This Lamb appears to have been offered as a sacrifice. He seems meek and gentle, yet there is about him a power and greatness that seems more like a lion. He is standing, which means he is alive, but he appears to have been slain, which means he once was dead. The Lamb bears on his body the marks of death, but he is alive. Thus anyone who looks at him knows that he was once offered as a sacrifice, and because he is standing, they know that he has come back from the dead.

As you watch and wonder, the Lamb comes to the throne and takes the scroll from the one who sits on it. The thought comes quickly that the Lamb can take the scroll because he is worthy and he is worthy because he was slain and he is able to take the scroll because, though he was dead, he has come back to life. At that moment the silence in heaven is broken as millions of angels begin to sing together: *'Worthy is the Lamb, who was slain, to receive power and wealth and wisdom and strength and honor and glory and praise!"* (Rev. 5:12). Then an answering chorus seems to rise from every corner of the universe: *"To him who sits on the throne and to the Lamb be praise and honor and glory and power, for ever and ever!"* (Rev. 5:13). "Amen!" cry the four living creatures

(v. 14). You fall on your face before the Lamb, lost in wonder, love, and praise.

The Mysterious Scroll

This description of heaven comes from Revelation 5. At the center of the action is a scroll with seven seals. When the seven seals are opened, they bring forth various judgments on the earth. When the seventh seal is opened, it contains seven trumpets of judgment. When the seventh trumpet sounds, it brings forth seven bowls of judgment. The seals, trumpets, and bowls describe the end-time catastrophes that will come upon the earth in the last days before the return of Jesus Christ to set up his kingdom. The remainder of the Book of Revelation describes those convulsive judgments that will be like the death throes of the present age and the birth pangs of the coming kingdom of the Christ. As one age dies in agony, another age is born.

The Book of Revelation nowhere precisely identifies the scroll. A variety of suggestions have been put forth. Certainly the scroll contains within it those final judgments, but that does not exhaust its meaning. During the Roman Empire, deeds or contracts were often sealed with seven seals. This included marriage contracts, rental and lease agreements, contract bills, and bonds.[2] Perhaps this scroll is the title-deed to the earth and the convulsive judgments describe the events that prepare the earth to receive its rightful owner. If so, then what was lost by Adam when he sinned has now been reclaimed and redeemed by Jesus Christ.

That explains why no one but Christ could take the scroll. The apostle John mentions the three great realms—in heaven, on earth, and under the earth—yet no one was found worthy.

No angel could open it.
No earthly ruler could open it.
No spirit creature could open it.
No demon could open it.
Not even Satan himself could open it.

But Jesus can take the scroll. The Lamb who was slain is now the Lion of the tribe of Judah. He has triumphed over death and hell and all the forces Satan could throw against him. Only a worthy victor could take the scroll and open it. He has fought the fight, won the battle, and now the spoils of war belong to him.

Stop and think about this great point. The Lamb has already won the battle. It's over. He's won. The victory is his. From God's point of view, Satan is already defeated.

I've never forgotten ten amazing days in Pignon, Haiti, when our missionary team led an evangelistic crusade during the week just before the national voodoo festival. The turning point came on Tuesday night when I preached on "Who Is Greater—Satan or Jesus?" That's a big issue in Haiti because so many people practice voodoo and live in fear of Satan's power. During my message I retold the story of how Satan tried to kill Jesus when he was born, how he tempted him in the wilderness, how Satan entered Judas and caused him to betray Christ, how the evil rulers plotted against Christ and finally nailed him to the cross. Down in hell, a party broke out—singing, shouting, laughing, cheering. The Son of God had finally been defeated. In heaven, an awesome silence.

But on Easter Sunday morning, something happened inside the tomb. In the place where death reigned, a tiny sound. A movement, a deep sigh, a fluttering heart comes back to life, blood courses through the veins, the color returns, the fingers begin to move, then the arms and the legs, and suddenly Jesus stood up and walked out of the tomb, alive from the dead!

Down in hell, shocked silence, then wild screams, shrieks of terror, wailing, mourning, gnashing of teeth. In heaven and across the universe, the people of God began to cheer, the angels lifted their voices, the trumpets began to sound, all creation shouted the good news. Jesus Christ has come back from the dead!

When I said those words in Haiti, the congregation began to clap and cheer. "If you're following Satan," I said, "you're following a defeated foe. You're following a loser. But if you follow Jesus, you're following the greatest winner in the history of the universe. He's the undisputed champion. He took on the pretender and knocked him out cold!"

That's what Revelation 5 means when it says that Christ has triumphed. He won the battle. It's over. The victory is his. Therefore, he and he alone is worthy to open the scroll and break the seven seals.

The Lion Who Is a Lamb

Who is this Lion who is a Lamb? He is standing because he is alive from the dead. He bears on his body the marks of his suffering. He is in the center of the throne and thus equal with God the Father. He is surrounded by the four living creatures and the elders and is the object of their worship. He has seven horns, symbolizing his complete authority. He has seven eyes that together represent the fullness of the Holy Spirit.

Who is this Lion who looks like a Lamb? He is none other than Jesus Christ, the Son of God. He is a Lion in that he is the mighty King of all kings. He is a Lamb because he was offered up as a sacrifice for the sins of the world. A mighty Lion! A meek Lamb!

Christ the Lion is victorious because Christ the Lamb made the perfect sacrifice.

The Lamb speaks of his First Coming.

The Lion speaks of his Second Coming.

He came once as a Lamb offered for the sins of the world. He came to save us from our sins. He came meek and mild. He comes again as a Lion to judge the world and to deliver his people. The key event occurs in Revelation 5:7 when the Lamb takes the scroll from the one who sits on the throne. This signals that his victory is complete and that the final events of history are now about to unfold. The rest of the Book of Revelation follows from this symbolic gesture. From this point on, the Lamb is in control of all events. Although much suffering will come to the earth, although death and destruction, famine and pestilence run unchecked, although the Antichrist will have his day, the Lamb still holds the scroll. It never leaves his hands.

Once again we are reminded that all of life is in God's hands. When the very worst that can happen does indeed happen, we may ask, "Where is God?" But he is there, where he has always been, on the throne of the universe, watching over every detail of life. Nothing escapes his gaze. While the world seems to be falling apart, he holds the scroll. While the nations rise up against one another, he holds the scroll. While famine spreads from the Sahara to the Middle East, while armies march toward Armageddon, while Babylon the Great rears its ugly head once again, he holds the scroll.

In the midst of perplexing circumstances, let this thought bring you hope: The Lamb holds the scroll in his hand. He controls the destiny of the nations. Nothing is out of control. Everything—even the most despicable evil—is under his control.

Verses 9 and 10 contain a short course in Christian theology. You might call it the Theology of Redemption. *"You are worthy to take the scroll and to open its seals, because you were slain, and with your blood you purchased men for God from every tribe and language and people and nation. You have made them to be a kingdom and priests to serve our God, and they will reign on the earth."* First, there is the cost of redemption: "your blood." Then there is the act of redemption: "You purchased men for God." Then the extent of redemption: "From every tribe and language and people and nation." Then the result of redemption: "You made them to be a kingdom and priests." Finally, there is the consummation of redemption: "They will reign on the earth."

It is a song of praise for redemption. Jesus Christ had to die, and his blood must be shed, but it was for a purpose. The blood of Christ was the purchase price of a great host of men and women for God. Jesus came as God's purchasing agent to the earth. He searched through every tribe, every nation, every region, every continent, every country, every state, every province, every city, every village, going up and down every street, searching out men and women he might purchase for God.

Four Truths About Heaven

John's vision in Revelation 5 teaches us many important facts about heaven. Here are four truths that will help us keep our eyes firmly fixed on our eternal home.

1. Heaven is a real place populated with real people and living beings of unimaginable splendor. There are many things we do not know and many symbols are beyond our comprehension. But this much is clear. There is a place called heaven, a real place, an actual destination—just like Singapore, Nairobi, Zurich, or New Orleans. This is a hugely important point because for many Christians heaven seems vague and unreal, like some shimmering fairy-tale land that doesn't really exist. We are so tied to the earth that we think of this world as the "real world." But this world is passing away (1 John 2:17). There is another world of spiritual reality centered around the throne of God in heaven. That world is the "real world" because it alone will last forever. The Book of Revelation puts heaven and earth in proper perspective. Against the splendor of this awesome vision, "earth is revealed to be temporary and transitory, and its glory and glitter are tarnished."[3]

Who will make up the population of heaven? Revelation 5:9 tells us that with his blood Christ *"purchased men for God from every tribe and language and people and nation."* God will not be defeated. There will be no empty thrones in heaven. God will not be satisfied with a handful in heaven while the devil gets the majority. What kind of salvation would that be? Many will be saved from every nation. God has a quota, and the quota will be met. This ought to encourage us about the power of the gospel, about the magnitude of God's heart, and the universality of the church. In this scene we have the end to all sectarianism, the end to all pessimism, and the end to evangelistic discouragement. It's easy for us to say, "Us four and no more," as if somehow sinners are so evil they can't be saved nowadays. Away with all such poor-meism and unbelief! I realize that as we look around at the cultural decline, it's tempting to conclude that the bad guys are winning. They aren't. God keeps score in his own way. And even when it looks like he's losing, he's not. He only appears to be trailing. But in the end, God wins. And he wins big. There will be more people in heaven than we have dreamed possible, because our God is greater than our limited imagination.

This picture of a vast multitude also teaches us that in the end every geographic barrier that separates us will be swept away. Every prejudice will be gone. Every bit of human strife will be left behind, and partisan bickering will simply be forgotten. What a good day that will be when all God's children meet together around the throne.

But note that we keep our individuality in heaven. The redeemed are saved from every nation, tribe, language, and people group. Just as Jesus retained the marks of his earthly suffering after his resurrection, even so we will retain our personal and group identities. The saints are all redeemed, but they are not homogenized. What language will we speak in heaven? Answer: All of them. In heaven we will hear English, Spanish, Urdu, Portuguese, French, Italian, Russian, Swahili, Hausa, Finnish, Yiddish, Hindi, Guarani, Hebrew, Arabic, Turkish, Korean, Japanese, Chinese, to name just a few. Although I can't prove this, I believe each person will speak whatever language(s) they knew on earth and the rest of us will understand everything that is said. That is, I may hear someone speaking Arabic and I will know it is Arabic and I will understand it even though right now I can't speak Arabic at all. In heaven I believe we will understand all the languages we hear, just as the early believers did on the Day of Pentecost in Acts 2:1–13.

And if you think about it, this answers the oft-repeated question: Will we know our loved ones in heaven? The answer is yes. If in heaven I am still joined to my nation, my tribe, my own people (Rev. 7:9–17), and if I still speak my own language, how can it be that I will be a stranger to my own loved ones? Such a thought is impossible. Those relationships on earth that were sanctified by saving grace will continue for all eternity, becoming deeper and more precious as the ages roll on. Consider an aged couple who have walked together for fifty-five years, facing all the joys and trials of life hand in hand. Will they say a fond farewell to this life, only to become strangers in the next? It is inconceivable, impossible, and against the words of Revelation 5. It cannot be true. Those I love in this life I will love more deeply in the next. And that love will be returned in a purer form in heaven because it is not mixed with base desires and earthly weakness.

What a glorious picture of heaven this is. There is heavenly harmony, a symphony of praise. Every day is a holiday (literally a "holy day") in heaven.

2. *The glory of heaven is the Lamb—Jesus Christ, whose victory is celebrated without end.* John is very specific about the geography of heaven. He saw the Lamb standing "in the center" of the throne. Jesus is the focal point of heaven and the center of all attention. It is not too much to say that without Jesus there would be no heaven at all. And without him none of us would ever have a chance to go there. As the famous hymn says, "When we've been there ten thousand years, bright shining as the sun, we've no less days to sing his praise than when we've first begun."

3. *The atmosphere of heaven is praise and worship.* Nothing there is dull and lifeless. No one falls asleep or looks at his watch. There no one worries about getting out on time. In heaven you never shovel snow off the walk or struggle to find a parking place. There the heater always works, the organ is always in tune, the choir cannot make a mistake, and if the preacher is long-winded, no one notices because a thousand years is like a day.

Children sometimes wonder if heaven will be boring. After all, it sounds like one really long church service. Who wants to go to church forever? Many adults have secretly wondered the same thing. What do the saints do in heaven? Here is my answer to the question: They stand, they sing, and they serve. They celebrate a great victory, they serve in God's temple, they see God on his throne, and they follow the Lamb everywhere. On one level I am sure we will never grow bored doing that. After all, we will never come to the end of God. And we'll never come to the end of the universe. And we will never run out of things to learn.

I find it helpful to think of it this way. *In heaven all our gifts and talents will finally be used.* Here on earth so many things hold us back. Sometimes circumstances keep us from doing what we know deep inside we could do if only someone would give us the chance. The expectations of others keep us hemmed in. The demands of daily life keep us from being all that we could be. Physical limitations hamper us. There are those among us who want to sing and love to sing, but there is no one to listen. Others want to paint, to cook, to write, to design, and to lead. Think of your dreams and hopes and aspirations and ponder how few have been fully realized. In heaven you will have ample time to develop them all—and in ways that would startle you if you knew about it now. *We will take all our gifts and talents and put them at the disposal of the Lord, and for all eternity we will find ourselves growing and learning and all the while celebrating the amazing grace of our Sovereign God.*

We will live there, work there, serve there, rejoice there, fellowship there, eat there, and serve throughout the regions of the universe at the bidding of our great God and his Son the Lord Jesus Christ. Yes, we will see our loved ones in heaven. Yes, the redeemed of all the ages will be there. But the central fact will not be reminiscing about the old times on earth. The central fact will be that Jesus himself is there—the Lamb that was slain on our behalf.

4. *A true vision of heaven gives us hope to face the difficulties of this life*. Beginning in Revelation 6, we see in vivid detail the horror that is outpoured on the earth as the seals are opened. Above it all stands the Lamb who is opening the scroll and reclaiming the earth that is rightfully his.

It is sometimes alleged that you can believe too much in heaven. The saying goes, "He's so heavenly minded that he's no earthly good." I beg to differ. I've never met anyone who remotely meets that definition. Only the truly heavenly minded can do any lasting good on the earth. It is precisely because we believe in heaven that we, like Moses of old, shun the riches of Egypt, choosing rather to suffer affliction with the people of God. We do what we do precisely because we're going to heaven and we know it. It would do us good to return to Revelation 5 at least once a year and contemplate the wondrous scenes opened for us. We would be less prone to complain, less tempted to give up, less inclined to dabble in the things of the world.

One final word. The glory of heaven is Jesus. As the long ages roll on, we will never tire of singing his praise. We will see him, still bearing the marks of his suffering on our behalf. In that day the redeemed saints of God will sing with one united voice, "All hail the power of Jesus' name, let angels prostrate fall. Bring forth the royal diadem and crown him Lord of all." Let the song begin in your heart this very day.

Going Deeper

1. Read Revelation 5 aloud. How is this passage the answer to self-centered worship and pessimistic evangelism?

A Truth to Remember: *If you follow Jesus, you're following the greatest winner in the history of the universe.*

2. Why is the dual image of Christ as a lion and a lamb so appropriate? What do we learn from each image?

3. Why is the Lamb the only one worthy to open the scroll? What happens on earth as the scroll is slowly unfolded? What is the significance of the Lamb holding the scroll as it unfolds?

4. Read Revelation 7:9–17. What additional information does it contain about the population of heaven and about our heavenly activities?

5. Spend a few minutes in a time of personal worship. Sing hymns and choruses that focus on the Lord Jesus Christ. Think of this as "practicing for heaven."

A closing word:
Lingering at the foot of the cross

ONE SUNDAY MORNING AFTER the final worship service had ended, a woman approached me with an unusual question: "Do you know why I'm here?" I had never seen her before, had no idea who she was, and therefore didn't know the answer to her question. But I did notice the tears in her eyes. "Why am I crying?" she asked. She had been raised in another faith and knew very little about evangelical Christianity. But "something" had drawn her, and when we invited people to come forward for a time of prayer, she had responded, slowly and hesitantly. Later I discovered that although she had gone to church as a child, she had wandered far from her religious training. I didn't have to convince her that she was a sinner. She knew that already, by conviction and by deep personal experience.

With her permission, I will share just a bit of her own story. As you will see, she speaks as a new believer whose life is in the process of being transformed by Jesus Christ.

I am thirty-nine years old, and I have a four-and-one-half-year-old son. I am not married and have never been married. I smoke cigarettes and swear I'm going to quit. I even try sometimes. Sometimes I use bad language and then I swear I won't swear anymore. When stress gets the best of me, I sometimes have a quick temper and snap at those closest to me—even my little boy. Sometimes I forget to say the blessing before I eat and know that I am not setting a good example for my son. Sometimes I hate my job and forget to be grateful that I have one. Sometimes I lose patience with my parents who are getting older and who are wonderful to me and my son. Sometimes I just don't feel like praying and doing the right thing. Sometimes I whine and complain and let self-pity and envy enter my heart. These are just some of my defects of character, some of my daily sins. And, if you think that's bad, you cannot begin to imagine how much better I am than I used to be.

And, most important, with all of these faults, some great, some small, God loves me and I am going to heaven. A long time ago a man named Jesus Christ died on a hill, on a cross, with nails driven through his hands and feet, for me and for you so that we may be forgiven our sins. I have accepted Jesus Christ as my Savior and that is all that God has asked of any of us. God knows my heart. He knows how badly I want to do better. And he also knows that in spite of all the many faults I have today, they are a tremendously vast improvement on the way I used to be.

The way she used to be includes drugs, alcohol abuse, repeated sexual promiscuity, attempted suicide, and shamanism. For years she lived in fear that God would punish her for her sins. She prayed, but nothing seemed to change, and the pit was so deep that she felt trapped with no way of escape. But still she yearned for a new life.

I was hungry to know God. I was hungry to teach my son about God. But I didn't know what to do. So I started praying "God, please show me the way—show me the way to you." I prayed that many times a day.

The turning point came in an unexpected way:

One night I was driving home in rush-hour traffic on the freeway and listening to a Christian radio station. I can't tell you exactly who was speaking, but *someone was talking about the crucifixion and I didn't know what happened—I started crying and saying something like, "Oh Jesus, please forgive me for sinning against you, I am so sorry, after all that you did for me, look what I have done to you—I know who you are now."* And the feeling in that car was overwhelming. I didn't know what was going on then—but I know now. *The Holy Spirit swooped down on me, he called me to Jesus and I came.* Isn't that something—the most incredible experience of my life and it happened in a rush-hour traffic jam on a cold night in November. I left the house that morning and came back that night a different woman—and I had no clue what was going on.

She ended her testimony with these words:

> Please don't be afraid to be a friend to someone
> who is living in sin. They need you more than
> those of us who are no longer in pain. Nobody
> wants to suffer like sinners suffer. They just need
> God, and God must use us to reach them. They are
> spiritually blind, and we have to help them see. To
> quote my favorite song which seems so very appro-
> priate, and which in one sentence certainly sums
> up what has happened since I came to Christ:
> "Amazing grace, how sweet the sound, that saved a
> wretch like me! I once was lost but now I'm found,
> was blind but now I see."

It was a vision of the cross that changed her life. What rules
and good intentions and tears and years of sincere resolutions
couldn't do, the cross did in one shining moment of repentance
and faith. When she saw the cross and the one who died there,
and when she realized who he was and why he died, and that he
did it for her, that moment, that vision, that revelation of God's
love radically changed her life from the inside out.

Now when she writes letters, she signs them, "Lingering at the
foot of the cross." That seems like a good place to end this book.
It is the cross that saves us, the cross that changes us, the cross
that gives us hope. And one day when we see Jesus, we will bow
before him, seeing in his hands and feet the very marks of his
death that gave us life. That day is not yet. Until then, we linger
at the foot of the cross where we behold the wonder and mystery
of the Lamb who died for us.

notes

Chapter 1, "Forgiving the Unforgivable"

1. Scholars debate the chronology of the crucifixion. For a discussion of the various options, see Harold W. Hoehner, *Chronological Aspects of the Life of Christ* (Grand Rapids: Zondervan Publishing House, 1977).

Chapter 3, "Final Words of a Family Man"

1. James Montgomery Boice and Philip Graham Ryken, *The Heart of the Cross* (Wheaton, Ill.: Crossway Books, 1999), 29–31.

Chapter 4, "The Forsaken Christ"

1. William L. Lane notes that crucifixions "were marked by screams of rage and pain, wild curses and the shouts of indescribable despair by the unfortunate victim." *Commentary on the Gospel of Mark* (Grand Rapids: Eerdmans, 1974), 572.

2. F. F. Bruce, *The Hard Sayings of Jesus* (Downers Grove, Ill.: InterVarsity, 1983), 248.

3. Ira D. Sankey, ed., *Sacred Songs & Solos* (London: Morgan & Scott, n.d.), 128.

Chapter 6, "Paid in Full"

1. Matthew Henry, *Commentary on the Whole Bible*, vol. 5, *Matthew to John* (Old Tappan, N.J.: Revell, n.d.), 1201.

2. Merrill Tenney, *Expositor's Bible Commentary*, vol. 9, *John-Acts* (Grand Rapids: Zondervan, 1981), 185.

Chapter 7, "A Time to Die"

1. For a discussion of the medical aspects of crucifixion, see W. D. Edwards, W. J. Gabel, and F. E. Hosmer, "On the Physical Death of Jesus Christ," *JAMA*. 255 (11), 1455–63, 1986.

Chapter 8, "Where Grace and Wrath Meet: What the Cross Meant to God"

1. D. A. Carson, *Basics for Believers* (Grand Rapids: Baker, 1996), 38.

2. The Phil Donahue quotes come from Erwin Lutzer, *Why the Cross Can Do What Politics Can't* (Eugene, Ore.: Harvest House, 1999), 111.

3. John Piper, "God's Invincible Purpose: Foundations for Full Assurance #3," 22 March 1992; and Phil Campbell, "The Real Solution," n.d.

4. Gareth Flanery, "What God Did at the Cross of Golgotha," n.d.

5. Charles Haddon Spurgeon, "Justification by Grace," 5 April 1857.

Chapter 9, "He Became Sin for Us: What the Cross Meant to Christ"

1. Charles Haddon Spurgeon, "The Heart of the Gospel," 18 July 1886.

2. Dave Redick, "The Good News: Hear It Again for the First Time," n.d.

3. *Biblical Illustrator: 2 Corinthians* (Grand Rapids: Baker, n.d.), 316–23.

4. I am not suggesting that the Christian faith does not commend itself to rational thinking or that it doesn't "make sense." In the end nothing is more rational than to believe the word of the one who created you. I am simply pointing out that apart from the knowledge of God, no one can truly understand the gospel.

5. Ray Stedman, "The Word for This Hour," 9 December 1979.

Chapter 10, "'One Little Word Shall Fell Him': What the Cross Means to Satan"

1. Charles Simeon, *Expository Outlines on the Whole Bible*, vol. 1, *Genesis-Leviticus* (Grand Rapids: Baker, 1988 reprint), 36.

2. Charles Spurgeon, "Christ the Conqueror of Satan," 26 November 1876.

3. F. E. Marsh, *The Greatest Theme in the World* (New York: Alliance Press Company, 1908), 123.

4. John Stott, *The Cross of Christ* (Downers Grove, Ill.: InterVarsity, 1986).

5. Michael Green, *I Believe in Satan's Downfall* (Grand Rapids: Eerdmans, 1981), 213–14.

6. F. E. Marsh, *Greatest Theme*, 125.

7. Erwin Lutzer, *Serpent of Paradise* (Chicago, Ill.: Moody, 1996), 98.

Chapter 11, "The Fool on the Hill: What the Cross Means to the World"

1. John R. W. Stott, *The Cross of Christ*, 19–24.

2. D. A. Carson, *Basics for Believers*, 46.

3. Erwin W. Lutzer, *Why the Cross Can Do What Politics Can't* (Eugene, Ore.: Harvest House, 1999), 86–93.

Chapter 12, "Our Crucified God: What the Cross Means to the Church"

1. Kenneth Woodward, "2000 Years of Jesus," *Newsweek*, 29 March 1999, 52.

2. Robert E. Coleman, *Written in Blood* (Old Tappan, N.J.: Revell, 1972), 111–12.

3. David Wilkerson, "They Have Done Away with the Cross!" 23 December 1996.

4. Merrill Tenney, *Who's the Boss?* (Wheaton, Ill.: Victor, 1980), 80.

5. Dietrich Bonhoeffer, *The Cost of Discipleship*, 2d ed., trad. R. H. Fuller (New York: Macmillan, 1959), 79.

6. Charles Edward White, "Small Sacrifices," *Christianity Today*, 22 June 1992, 32–33.

7. James M. Campbell, "The Dynamic of Christianity," *Homiletic Review*, 1908, 181.

Chapter 13, "Free at Last! The Cross and Our Sin"

1. John Watson, *The Doctrines of Grace* (London: Hodder and Stoughton, 1900), 65.

2. James Montgomery Boice, *Romans*, vol. 2, *The Reign of Grace—Romans 5–8* (Grand Rapids: Baker, 1992), 663-64.

3. Ibid., 670.

4. Ibid., 647–48.

Chapter 14, "Worthy Is the Lamb: The Cross in Heaven"

1. William R. Moody, *The Life of D. L. Moody* (Murfreesboro, Tenn.: Sword of the Lord, reprint, n.d.), 552-53.

2. Robert L. Thomas, *Revelation 1–7: An Exegetical Commentary* (Chicago: Moody, 1992), 378.

3. John F. Walvoord, *The Revelation of Jesus Christ* (Chicago, Ill.: Moody, 1966), 121.

Special Note

If you would like to contact the author, you can reach him in the following ways:

By letter:
    Ray Pritchard
    Calvary Memorial Church
    931 Lake Street
    Oak Park, IL 60301

By E-mail: PastorRay@cmcop.org

Via the Internet: www.cmcop.org